THE CAMBRIDGE B   Y

NEW ENGLISH BIBLE

GENERAL EDITORS

P. R. ACKROYD, A. R. C. LEANEY, J. W. PACKER

THE PASTORAL LETTERS

THE PASTORAL
LETTERS

COMMENTARY ON
THE FIRST AND SECOND LETTERS TO TIMOTHY
AND THE LETTER TO TITUS

BY

ANTHONY TYRRELL HANSON
Professor of Theology, University of Hull

CAMBRIDGE
AT THE UNIVERSITY PRESS
1966

PUBLISHED BY
THE SYNDICS OF THE CAMBRIDGE UNIVERSITY PRESS

Bentley House, 200 Euston Road, London, N.W. 1
American Branch: 32 East 57th Street, New York, N.Y. 10022
West African Office: P.M.B. 5181, Ibadan, Nigeria

©

CAMBRIDGE UNIVERSITY PRESS

1966

Printed in Great Britain at the University Printing House, Cambridge
(Brooke Crutchley, University Printer)

LIBRARY OF CONGRESS CATALOGUE
CARD NUMBER: 66–11281

GENERAL EDITORS' PREFACE

The aim of this series is to provide the text of the New English Bible closely linked to a commentary in which the results of modern scholarship are made available to the general reader. Teachers and young people preparing for such examinations as the General Certificate of Education at Ordinary or Advanced Level in Britain, and similar qualifications elsewhere have been especially kept in mind. The commentators have been asked to assume no specialized theological knowledge, and no knowledge of Greek and Hebrew. Bare references to other literature and multiple references to other parts of the Bible have been avoided. Actual quotations have been given as often as possible.

Within these quite severe limits each commentator will attempt to set out the main findings of recent New Testament scholarship, and to describe the historical background to the text. The main theological content of the New Testament will also be critically discussed.

Much attention has been given to the form of the volumes. The aim is to produce books each of which will be read consecutively from first to last page. The introductory material leads naturally into the text, which itself leads into the alternating sections of commentary. By this means it is hoped that each book will be easily read and remain in the mind as a unity.

The series is prefaced by a volume—*Understanding the New Testament*—which outlines the larger historical background, says something about the growth and transmission of the text, and answers the question 'Why should we study the New Testament?' Another volume —*New Testament Illustrations* —contains maps, diagrams and photographs.

P.R.A.
A.R.C.L.
J.W.P.

CONTENTS

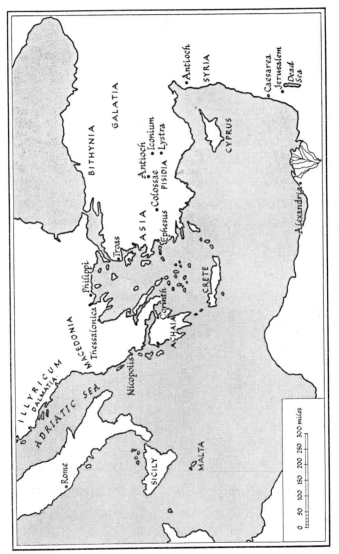

PLACES MENTIONED IN THE PASTORAL LETTERS

THE PASTORAL
LETTERS

✳   ✳   ✳   ✳   ✳   ✳   ✳   ✳   ✳   ✳   ✳   ✳   ✳

WHY ARE THE PASTORAL LETTERS DIFFERENT?

They certainly are different from the other Pauline letters, and
we cannot hope to understand them unless we begin by asking
why they are different. All through the centuries since they
were first written they have stood apart from the other letters
of Paul. The actual description 'Pastoral Epistles' is only
about three hundred and fifty years old. Thomas Aquinas
(died 1274) described 1 Timothy as 'a pastoral textbook', and
this phrase pin-points one of the features that makes the
Pastorals different from the other letters. They contain advice
about how to run the Church such as we do not find in exactly
the same way in other letters of Paul. Paul does indeed, in
1 Corinthians for example, give plenty of advice on problems
which have cropped up in the life of the Church in Corinth.
But this is more detailed and more fitted to one local situation
than anything we find in the Pastorals. Another feature which
makes them different is that they are written apparently for
the benefit of individual church leaders, Timothy and Titus.
We do, it is true, have one other example of a letter written by
Paul to an individual, the letter to Philemon. But we have
only to read Philemon over once (it does not run to more than
twenty-five verses in all) to see for ourselves how very different it is from any of the Pastoral letters. It is written to deal
with one particular historical situation. It contains no *general*
advice at all. It does begin with a greeting to the Church in
Philemon's house, but after that it is wholly concerned with a
personal matter between Paul and Philemon.

So far we have only dealt with the differences in form and

main contents between the Pastoral letters and the others.
And one could quite reasonably say that these differences are
accounted for by the fact that we do not happen to have any
other letters of Paul written to individual church leaders.
But we have still to mention the most important differences
of all: these are differences in style, vocabulary, and actual
thought. Style is something which it is very difficult to identify; yet a careful, sensitive reading of the Pastoral letters must
leave one with the impression that the style is not just that of
the other Pauline letters. It is less enthusiastic, less fiery, less
emphatic than what we meet in 2 Corinthians or Colossians,
for example. There are fewer references to the great central
beliefs of Christianity, very few indeed to the Cross. It is
true that there are very few such references in Philemon, and
not so very many in 2 Thessalonians. But, once again, the
matter must be decided by reading the works concerned.
Read over Philemon and the two Thessalonian letters, and
then ask yourself: is this the same style as the Pastorals?

Vocabulary is something which is best left to the experts,
and the experts nowadays tend to hand the problem on to the
computer. But we can easily point to a number of key words
in the Pastorals which simply do not occur in the other Pauline
letters: there is *eusebeia*, for example, translated by the N.E.B.
as 'religion'. It is a favourite word in the Pastorals; it carries
an overtone of 'piety', 'god-fearingness', almost 'middle-
class religion'. Paul never uses it in any of his other letters.
Or we could point to the title *Sōtēr*, 'Saviour'. In all his other
works Paul only uses it once, in Phil. 3: 20, of Christ. But in
the Pastorals it is his favourite epithet both for God and Christ.
Again, we could ask why is God called 'Dynast' in 1 Tim.
6: 15 (the N.E.B. rather loosely turns it into a verb: 'God . . .
holds sway'). Or why is he called 'King of all worlds' in
1 Tim. 1: 17? These are words which are used for God in
Jewish writings of the period between the Old Testament and
the New, and also in the earliest Christian writings outside the
New Testament. But they are never found in Paul's other

writings. We could look at it the other way round, and ask why Paul never calls Christ 'the Son' in the Pastorals, while it is one of his most usual ways of referring to Christ in his other works. These words are not far-fetched ones, only suitable to one particular set of circumstances. They are words which one would expect a man to use whenever he wrote about Christianity. From these few examples, therefore, it can be seen that the vocabulary of the Pastorals needs some explaining.

It is the same with the thought of the Pastorals: we want to know, for example, how it is that Paul can write about the Law as he does in 1 Tim. 1: 8–11. In the rest of his writings, and especially in Galatians and Romans, the Law is a power hostile to man, originally provided by God because of man's sinfulness, but now, by the coming of Christ, made out of date and irrelevant for those who accept God's offer of friendship. In this passage in 1 Timothy the Law is something much less complicated, it is simply that which condemns evildoers. Why this remarkable change of doctrine? Or again: in all his other writings Paul opposes false teaching by arguing against it, showing how it conflicts with basic Christian beliefs. But in the Pastorals, though he spends much time condemning false teaching, he does not argue. He appeals to an existing body of teaching as a treasure committed to the Church, but he does not argue as to the respective merits of the true and false teaching. On the contrary, he discourages argument. These are two outstanding instances which suggest that, in the sphere of their actual thought-content also, the Pastorals are different from the rest of Paul's letters.

SOME SUGGESTED ANSWERS TO THE QUESTION

Naturally, various attempts have been made to account for these striking differences. Only three solutions are possible, and only one of them can be right. We must look at these three:

1. *Paul wrote these letters in his old age*

The defenders of this solution point to the obvious fact that, as far as we know, nobody ever doubted Paul's authorship of these letters until the question was raised two hundred years ago. They claim to be written by Paul; they contain many references to details of Paul's life and circumstances; they are addressed to real, historical people about whom we read in Acts and in Paul's undoubtedly genuine letters. They sometimes echo Paul's own language. In so far as there is a change of style and contents in them, say these scholars, this can be explained by a consideration of the circumstances in which they were written. Paul was old and tired, and had lost his earlier fire and energy. He was probably in prison and in very close confinement in Rome. Scholars have pointed out the difficulties involved in letter-writing in ancient times even under the happiest conditions, and have suggested that Paul may have had to rely on the services of a secretary when he wrote the Pastorals. Perhaps the altered style and vocabulary are to be put to the account of the secretary. But the letters, such scholars insist, are Paul's in essence.

The case for full Pauline authorship is not completely convincing. Some people have even claimed that in the second century A.D. it was known that the Pastorals were not by Paul, on the grounds that Marcion did not know of them. Marcion was an unorthodox Christian teacher who lived in Rome about A.D. 140. He mentions the other Pauline letters, but not the Pastorals. But Marcion is not a reliable guide, as he did pick and choose among the New Testament Books recognized by orthodox Christians, and he may have known the Pastorals but rejected them for doctrinal reasons. Again, there is in existence a papyrus manuscript of the Pauline letters dating from about A.D. 250, known as $\mathfrak{P}^{46}$, which does not contain the Pastorals. (This Gothic $\mathfrak{P}$ is used by scholars to indicate a papyrus manuscript.) It is one of the earliest manuscripts of the New Testament we possess, so its evidence is important. But

4

it is incomplete, and, though it is very doubtful whether there would have been room for all three Pastoral letters in the missing portion, its evidence cannot be called conclusive. As for the suggestion that the style and the thought of Paul grew feebler as he grew older, this is not very flattering to Paul. There may be something in the secretary hypothesis, but how much is Paul and how much secretary? The Pastorals give the impression that the secretary more or less took command. A final objection to this theory lies in the difficulty of fitting the details of Paul's career which we learn from the Pastorals into the outline of his career as we know it from other sources.

2. *The Pastorals are not written by Paul at all, but by some other church leader who lived about fifty years after Paul's death*

This is not as startling a suggestion as it sounds, for we have at least one example in the New Testament of a letter which was written in these circumstances. This is 2 Peter, which is certainly not by Peter, but was written in Peter's name perhaps as late as A.D. 120. This solution explains all the differences from the rest of the Pauline letters: the teaching, style, and vocabulary are different because the writer was different. The champions of this view can point to several links between the Pastorals and Christian writings of the period A.D. 100–20 especially in the matter of vocabulary. The blanket condemnation of false teachers without argument is very like what we find in 2 Peter and in Jude (the latter probably belongs to the end of the first century). The suggestion is that some influential Christian teacher, probably in Asia Minor, wished to write a sort of handbook for local church leaders, and that he decided to issue it in Paul's name, both because as an admirer of Paul he believed he was maintaining Paul's teaching, and because he wished to lend Paul's authority to his work. It was a period when the Church was much harried by false teaching. This practice of issuing a book in the name of some revered figure of the past was an accepted convention at the time and would not have carried the suggestion of dishonesty that it would certainly incur today. Compare the way in which the first five Books of the Old Testament are attributed to Moses although it is quite certain that Moses did not write them.

There is much truth in this suggestion; indeed, as we have seen, it meets most of the difficulties. But it does not fully explain all the evidence. There are, for example, many personal details about Paul's life to be found in the Pastorals, especially in 2 Timothy 4. Rigorous upholders of the theory we are now discussing must maintain that these details are all invented by the author. This seems unlikely. It is true that by the middle of the second century plenty of fantastic legends about Paul had grown up, but only a few scholars would date the Pastorals as late as that. As we shall see, it is extremely difficult to date them after A.D. 110, and they are probably earlier. This hardly leaves time for so much apparently useless legend to have grown up. Most scholars who reject suggestion 1, therefore, are inclined to accept some form of suggestion 3.

3. *The Pastorals are a later writing, but they contain genuine fragments of Paul's letters*

This account of the Pastorals begins from suggestion 2, but explains most of the personal details by saying that they are genuine fragments of Pauline letters which came into the possession of the author of the Pastorals; he incorporated them into his three letters. This is the view adopted in this commentary, and is that of most modern English commentators.

It brings its own problems, however. In the first place, there is no agreement as to which fragments are by Paul. Some scholars accept a great deal as Pauline, some very little. This is a question of individual choice, and the particular selection adopted in this commentary will be clearly indicated in the text. It has been objected against this theory that Paul is hardly likely to have written brief notes to his friends; did Timothy and Titus receive postcards from their leader? This objection can be met by grouping all the allegedly Pauline material into two fragments, as has been done here. There is some evidence that small fragments of several different letters from Paul to the Church in Corinth are preserved in the work known to us as 2 Corinthians; for example, many scholars believe that 2 Cor. 6: 14 — 7: 1 represents a fragment of the first letter that Paul ever wrote to Corinth, and that it was at first preserved by the Corinthian Church inside the original manuscript of 2 Corinthians, and only later incorporated into the text of the letter. Another objection to this third theory is based on the difficulty, already mentioned on p. 5, of fitting such alleged details of Paul's career as we find in 2 Timothy 4 into his known life-history. But this difficulty can be met by following the very ancient hypothesis that Paul was released from prison after the two years mentioned in Acts 28: 30, and that he had a further missionary term of several years before being re-arrested and subsequently put to death.

THE DATING OF THE PASTORALS

Assuming, then, that the Pastorals were for the most part written after Paul's day, we have next to try to decide as accurately as we can when they were written. In this sort of question, the best way to proceed is to fix two dates within which the Pastorals must have been written, and then to see whether it is possible to decide on one particular year or years within that period. We begin therefore by suggesting the year A.D. 135. This is probably the year in which Polycarp, bishop of Smyrna, wrote a letter to the Church in Philippi, and it seems quite clear that he quotes 1 Tim. 6: 7 and 10 in this letter. He first says: 'The beginning of all difficulties is love of money', which sounds very like 'The love of money is the root of all evil things' (1 Tim. 6: 10); then he adds an almost verbatim quotation of 1 Tim. 6: 7: 'We brought nothing into the world, but we are not able to take anything with us either.' Polycarp, therefore, must have known 1 Timothy. As for a limit in the other direction, the author seems to refer to Acts 13: 50; and 14: 5, 19. These passages in Acts describe the dangers and persecutions encountered by Paul in Pisidian Antioch, Iconium, and Lystra, and to these 2 Tim. 3: 11 refers. The date of the publication of Acts is uncertain, but most scholars are inclined to put it at about A.D. 90. Thus we seem to have a period of roughly forty years in which to place the composition of the Pastorals, A.D. 95–135.

Can we be any more precise than this? It seems reasonable to suggest that we can. About the year A.D. 112, Pliny, the Roman governor of Bithynia wrote a letter to the Emperor Trajan asking his advice about the correct treatment of Christians. That letter has survived and we shall be referring to it in the course of the commentary. But for our purpose here it is sufficient to notice that Pliny gives us evidence that Christians were being persecuted in one part of Asia Minor about the year A.D. 112. Pliny himself did not begin the persecution of his own accord; it was rather forced on him by the activities of informers, who accused certain persons of being Christians. Pliny had to decide what to do with them. Trajan's reply has also survived: he says that Pliny must punish with death any who admit to being Christians and refuse to recant. Incidentally Pliny refers to certain individuals amongst those accused who said they had been Christians as long as twenty years ago, but had ceased to be so now. This suggests that in Bithynia at least there was persecution of Christians, coming, perhaps, at the end of a period of peace. Now in the Pastorals there is no hint whatever of persecution. If we assume, as all scholars do, that the Pastorals were intended for the Church in Asia Minor, probably in Ephesus, then it looks as if one must put the date of their composition decidedly before 112. Of course Ephesus was not in Pliny's province, but it is hard to believe that a persecution such as we read of in Pliny's letters could be taking place in Bithynia without producing any effect on the Church in the region of Ephesus. Incidentally, we may add here the

evidence of the Revelation of John. When Revelation was
written, there can be no doubt that persecution had been taking
place, and was still going on, in Asia Minor. Most scholars
agree with Irenaeus (died about A.D. 200) that Revelation was
written in the year 96. We must therefore put the Pastorals
some time later than this, to allow the expectation of persecution to die down. Thus we may reasonably suggest a date
round about the year 105 for the Pastorals.

Of course we could try to fit them into a period ten years
after the time of Pliny, say about A.D. 125. This would put
them in the first years of the Emperor Hadrian's reign, and
this seems to have been a time of comparative peace for Christians. But during this period Christians were still under the
threat of the same repressive action as Pliny had taken, and it
is hard to believe that this state of affairs would not be more
clearly reflected in the Pastorals. Besides, the date of A.D. 135
for Polycarp's letter is not absolutely certain. Some scholars
would put it as early as 117. This would of course virtually
compel us to adopt a date for the Pastorals of about 105.

There are three other small books in the New Testament
which seem to have been written in much the same circumstances as the Pastorals, very different though they are in style
and contents. These are the letters of John. Many scholars
would assign these letters to the years 100–5. It seems likely
that they were written to the Church in Asia Minor. They
show no sign of recent, present, or imminent persecution;
and, like the Pastorals, their author is greatly concerned to
oppose false teachers. It is even possible that they have one
more feature in common with the Pastorals: the author of the
letters of John (who calls himself the 'elder' or 'presbyter') is
disturbed by the behaviour of a certain leader in one of the
local Churches. This man, Diotrephes, is described by John
as 'their would-be leader' (see 3 John 9). Diotrephes seems
to be claiming a right to rule the local Church and to excom-
municate by his own authority those who do not acknowledge him. It has been suggested that what we have here is the

emergence in Diotrephes' local Church of the office of bishop
as it became known all over the Church later on in the second
century. Now, as we shall be seeing later, the Pastorals probably witness indirectly to the fact that the office of bishop has
recently been established in the churches to which they are
addressed. We may add to this that in the letters of Ignatius,
bishop of Antioch, which were written about A.D. 110, the
rule of bishops is established in Syria and Asia Minor, though
not, it seems, in Philippi or Rome. But the emphatic way in
which Ignatius defends the position of the bishop suggests
that this new institution was still under fire. Incidentally,
Ignatius' career is evidence of persecution in Syria, for he
wrote his seven letters while being conveyed as a condemned
criminal to Rome, where he was to suffer as a martyr.
Another point of contact with the time of Ignatius is the
reference to Jewish teachings in the Church which occur so
often in the Pastorals. Ignatius also was troubled by people
who wanted to bring the Church round again to Judaism.
All this evidence, indirect and inconclusive as it is when
examined piece by piece, does seem to build up a fair case for
dating the Pastorals at about A.D. 105.

THE DATING OF THE PAULINE MATERIAL

If we acknowledge any Pauline fragments in the Pastorals, we
should try to fit them into Paul's life-history. It is first necessary to state clearly which verses are to be treated in this commentary as genuinely from Paul's pen. They are as follows:

(*a*) 2 Tim. 1: 15–18;
(*b*) 2 Tim. 4: 9–21, omitting verse 18;
(*c*) Titus 3: 12–14.

Of these three, (*a*) tells us about Paul's experiences of his trial
in Rome; 1: 18 seems to imply that Timothy was in, or near,
Ephesus at the time that Paul wrote. (*b*) continues the same
theme, giving interesting information about the location of

various assistants of Paul. From 4: 12 we would guess that Timothy was not in Ephesus when this letter was written, but he must have been near enough to Ephesus to know what was going on there—if, that is, 2 Tim. 1: 18 is part of the same letter. A reasonable conjecture is that Timothy was at Colossae at the time. Three of Paul's companions mentioned in (*b*), Demas, Mark, and Luke, send their greetings to the Church in Colossae in Col. 4: 10, 14. Colossae was about 130 miles as the crow flies from Ephesus, near enough perhaps for Timothy to keep in touch, especially as we know that the two cities had continual contact with each other. We assume therefore that (*a*) and (*b*) belong to the same original letter written by Paul to Timothy from Rome, perhaps to Colossae. (*c*) cannot be part of the same letter, because it seems to have been written by Paul when he was at liberty to direct his own movements. Thus we are led to conclude that the author of the Pastorals had access to two letters, or fragments of letters, written by Paul.

As well as these, it is reasonable to suppose that the author had a certain amount of genuine historical information about Paul and Timothy. In other words, the historical information in the Pastorals is not entirely confined to the Pauline fragments. The author was writing, we have suggested, not more than forty years after Paul's death; and he was separated by a considerably shorter interval from the time of the deaths of Timothy and Titus. Of Titus we have no real information at all outside Paul's letters; but in the letter to the Hebrews there is a mention of Timothy. Heb. 13: 23 tells us that Timothy has recently been released; where from, or where, we do not know. But Hebrews was certainly written after the death of Paul, perhaps as much as ten or twenty years after. Thus, when we read in 2 Tim. 1: 5 that Timothy's mother was called Eunice and his grandmother Lois, it would be absurdly sceptical to deny that this is genuine information, not mere invention. The names of the false teachers Hymenaeus and Alexander in 1 Tim. 1: 20, and Philetus in 2 Tim. 2: 17, are no doubt names

of real people who were causing trouble by their unortho-
doxy, but it is by no means certain whether they belonged to
Paul's day or the author's. No doubt the tradition, reflected in
the letter to Titus, that Titus worked in Crete is historical. It
is difficult to make up one's mind about 1 Tim. 5: 23: 'Stop
drinking nothing but water; take a little wine for your digestion, for your frequent ailments.' As many editors have re-
marked, who would bother to invent a detail like this? If it is
genuine, it seems to be the only genuine Pauline fragment in
1 Timothy. We may add that the tradition of Timothy having
been ordained by Paul, mentioned in 2 Tim. 1: 6, is very
probably historical as well.

How does all this information fit into Paul's history as we
know it? Various efforts have been made to assign it to the
time when Paul was carrying on his missionary activity in
Asia Minor and Greece, before being sent as a prisoner to
Rome. He certainly was in prison for various terms during
that period. Several scholars have suggested that Paul was a
prisoner for some time in Ephesus (compare 1 Cor. 15: 32),
and that he wrote at least some of the 'Captivity' letters from
there. Others have pointed out that he spent two years in
prison in Caesarea (Acts 24: 27), and have tried to fit the
'Captivity' letters into this period. But no solution along
these lines has received general approval, and this sort of
arrangement always seems to involve cutting the genuine
material up into fragments of more than two letters.

We therefore fall back on the simple plan of assigning this
genuine material to what has been called 'the second missionary period', after Paul's release from captivity in Rome.
This is an ancient solution to the problem, but it does not meet
with much acceptance among modern scholars. The last
positive evidence we have about Paul is what we learn from
Acts 28. He was kept in Rome under comparatively light
confinement for two whole years after his arrival there. Then
—the curtain falls. The next evidence comes from the letter
of Clement, written probably in A.D. 96, by the representative

of the church authorities in Rome to the Church in Corinth. Clement implies that both Peter and Paul died as martyrs in Rome, and he seems to imply that Paul visited Spain in fulfilment of his intention expressed in Rom. 15: 24, 28. He says that Paul came 'to the limit (or goal) of the West'. This has been explained as meaning Rome, or else it has been rejected as Clement's guess. But it seems unjustified to reject it. The prevailing opinion today is that Paul was not released after the two years in Rome, but was kept in closer confinement and was ultimately put to death. In that case, our first fragment would have come from the period just before Paul's death. But if so, what of Colossians and Philemon? It would be very difficult to fit into that one Roman captivity all the comings and goings implied in Col. 4: 7–17, Philem. 23–4, and our first fragment. It seems much more reasonable to suppose that Paul was released after those two years, and that the events referred to in our first fragmentary letter ((*a*) and (*b*) above) took place during his free activity after release. There is, we must admit, very little evidence beyond what we find in the Pastorals that the second period of activity took place. But there is no evidence at all that he was put to death without being released after the two years were ended.

If this is where we put the activity referred to in 2 Tim. 1: 15–18; 4: 9–21, then we must assume that the letter which contained the references was written after Colossians and Philemon. In Philem. 22 Paul says: 'have a room ready for me, for I hope that, in answer to your prayers, God will grant me to you.' He was then expecting to be released soon. Colossians cannot be separated in time from Philemon. So the two must have been written before our fragmentary letter found in 2 Timothy. That letter was written by a man who was not expecting release, and may even have been preparing for a winter in prison (he sends for his cloak in 2 Tim. 4: 13). But there is no reason why Colossians and Philemon should not have been written towards the end of the two years' confinement of Acts 28. The assigning of dates to Paul's life is a

most difficult business, as so much is uncertain. A scheme of
dating which has respectable support is this:

A.D. 61: Paul arrives as a prisoner in Rome;
A.D. 63: he is released after two years in prison;
A.D. 67: having been re-arrested, he is executed in Rome.

This would allow plenty of time for a second period of activity,
including even a visit to Spain. Note that we are assuming, as
do many scholars today, that Philippians belongs to an earlier
period of Paul's life, and that the letter to the Ephesians is not
by Paul.

One small point remains: what of the third fragment,
Titus 3: 12–14? Here we must honestly say we do not know.
It could belong to the period before Paul's arrest in Jerusalem.
By the time he wrote Rom. 15: 19 Paul had already visited
Illyricum in Western Greece; Nicopolis, mentioned in Titus
3: 12, is also in this area. On the other hand it could belong
to the period of free activity we have supposed to have taken
place after his two years in Rome. We simply do not possess
the evidence to enable us to make up our minds about this.

Here is a brief summary of the argument for putting the
Pauline fragments in the second period of Paul's missionary
activity:

(1) If you take (*a*) and (*b*) as one letter, they seem to be directed to Timothy somewhere within range of Ephesus,
perhaps Colossae.

(2) It is impossible to fit all the details of such a letter within
the period of Paul's life up to his arrival in Rome.

(3) We therefore assume that Paul was released after two
years in Rome, and that the details in this letter refer to his
activity after that.

(4) But this means that Colossians and Philemon were
written at the end of the two-year imprisonment in Rome,
and that this letter (a fragment of which has survived in
2 Tim. 4) was written some time after his re-arrest and final
imprisonment, again in Rome.

A HANDBOOK FOR CHURCH LEADERS

One of the most puzzling features about the Pastorals is their miscellaneous nature. The author seems to move from personal exhortation to quoting verses from hymns; then back to advice about running the Church; then a warning against false teachers; then a list of qualities necessary for church leaders, and so on without apparent purpose. The reason for this is probably that the author was intending to write a sort of handbook for church leaders. He put it in the form of personal letters, and so introduced a certain amount of personal material. But the main aim was to give a model to leaders of the local Churches. In this respect Timothy and Titus are imaginary figures: not that they did not really live, but they are treated in the Pastorals as ideal figures, or what the local church leader ought to be like.

Once we approach the Pastorals with this in mind, we can better appreciate what the author was trying to do, and we will not condemn him for not being Paul. He himself was not a man of original genius as Paul was; indeed he cannot really be described as possessing a theology or system of thought of his own. This is the last thing he would have wanted. His great aim is not to introduce new teaching, but to persuade his readers to stand by the old. This is why he so often refers to 'sound teaching' (see 2 Tim. 1: 13; and compare 2 Tim. 4: 3; Titus 1: 9 'wholesome teaching'; Titus 1: 13 'sane belief'; 2: 1 'wholesome doctrine'). In fact it seems that he took his theological language from the prayer book and hymn book of his day. Scholars have come to the conclusion that most of the author's references to doctrine are really quotations, quotations from early Christian hymns, as in 1 Tim. 3: 16; 2 Tim. 2: 11–13; or from very early creeds, as in 1 Tim. 2: 5–6; or perhaps from a prayer used in the eucharist, as in 1 Tim. 1: 17; or even from the baptismal service, as probably in Titus 3: 4–7. He thus gives us interesting glimpses into the early Church at worship which we could ill afford to dispense with. Characteristic of the author's lack of originality is another feature of his work: these lists of desirable qualities for church leaders which he gives us do not seem to have come originally from Christian sources. They can be closely paralleled in the non-Christian literature of the author's day. For instance, the list of qualities required in a bishop given in I Tim. 3: 1–5 is very like a list of the qualities required in a good general which we find in a Greek writer called Onosander who wrote about A.D. 50. The author apparently took much of his moral teaching from contemporary pagan ethical writings.

If the Pastorals are a sort of handbook for church leaders, we can also understand what has puzzled many scholars in the past, the nature of the false teaching which the author condemns. Was it Jewish? It has many Jewish features; indeed the author refers to 'Jewish converts' and 'Jewish myths' in Titus I: 10 and 14. But the false teaching is also reminiscent of much Greek thought which took the form of Gnosticism. Gnosticism is a general title for a mixture of religion and philosophy that was undoubtedly in competition with Christianity during the second half of the first century A.D. It was highbrow; it often went in for elaborate systems of demi-gods or supernatural beings; it frequently demanded an extreme asceticism from its adherents, condemning the eating of certain foods, and even the practice of marriage itself. There are signs of all these things in the teaching which the author rejects. The explanation is surely that he wanted his readers to detect and oppose *all* current forms of false teaching. He was after all writing a handbook, and this is why his condemnations are general rather than specific.

It seems likely that the church leaders for whom he wrote were more or less in the position of bishops in their respective churches. His language on this point is vague: he speaks of 'elders' (literally 'presbyters') in the plural, and of 'the bishop' in the singular. But he can move from one to the other as if he were speaking of the same office, as in Titus I: 5–7.

Moreover his ideal Timothy and Titus are in the position of bishops, or rather archbishops, for they can appoint elders on their own authority. But this may be part of his ideal setting. The simplest explanation is that the author knew there had been no bishops in Paul's day, only groups of local ministers on the one hand, and the apostle with his fellow-missionaries on the other. But bishops had emerged in his day and he wants to speak to them, so he leaves it vague.

One more interesting element in the Pastorals is what we might call 'domestic codes'. This means sections containing advice on right behaviour for Christians in different social classes and relationships, such as elder women, younger men, slaves, and widows. We meet these in 1 Tim. 2: 9–15 (women); 5: 3–16 (widows); 6: 1–2 (slaves); Titus 2: 1–3 (elderly people); and verses 4–5 (younger women); verses 6–7 (younger men); verses 9–10 (slaves). These domestic codes are also found in other New Testament letters, especially Colossians and 1 Peter, and are a reminder of how much Christianity is a matter of family life. In the ancient world religion was often thought of as a purely public affair.

The author of the Pastorals is not a keen student of the Old Testament as Paul was. But he was still in close contact with Judaism, and it is not at all accurate to suggest, as some have done, that in his work we can see Christianity being overcome by Greek ways of thought and habits of life.

The author of the Pastorals, then, was no genius, but he probably provided what was most needed in his day, a workaday rule that would help Christians where help was most urgently required. How far his advice is relevant today, we shall judge for ourselves as we study his work.

It is not much use trying to decide the order in which the three letters were written. On the whole it seems likely that they were written in the order 2 Timothy, Titus, 1 Timothy. This would mean that the author put most Pauline material into his first letter, and had very little left by the time he came to I Timothy. But we do not know enough about the circumstances of writing to justify us in making a definite decision on this point.

✻   ✻   ✻   ✻   ✻   ✻   ✻   ✻   ✻   ✻   ✻   ✻   ✻

THE FIRST LETTER TO TIMOTHY

✳ In this letter the main themes are defence against error and the building up of the life of the Church. But it is most haphazard and miscellaneous, so no neat scheme will fit it. Passages that appear to be quotations from prayers or hymns or creeds are listed in bold type in this contents list.

✵   ✵   ✵   ✵   ✵   ✵   ✵   ✵   ✵   ✵   ✵   ✵   ✵

Church Order

ADDRESS

1 FROM PAUL, apostle of Christ Jesus by command of
2 God our Saviour and Christ Jesus our hope, to Timothy his true-born son in the faith.

Grace, mercy, and peace to you from God the Father and Christ Jesus our Lord.

✵ We should not be surprised at a rather formal beginning to what is supposed to be a personal letter. We live in an informal age; a hundred years ago children were taught to write to their father and mother as 'honoured parents'.

1. *Christ Jesus.* This rather than 'Jesus Christ' is more common in the Pastorals. In the rest of Paul's letters both forms are frequently found. Only very rarely does Paul use 'Christ' as a title meaning 'the anointed King', rather than as a personal name. In the Pastorals it always seems to be simply a name.

God our Saviour. The word *Saviour* is used ten times in the Pastorals (six times for God and four times for Christ). In the genuine Pauline letters it only occurs once, Phil. 3: 20 (but also once in Eph. 5: 23, which we are treating as not directly from Paul). The author of 2 Peter also shows a liking for the word; in one short letter he uses it five times for Christ. *Sōtēr* as applied to God is a word with a rich history. It was used by Greek-speaking Jews by the time of Christ at least; compare Ps. 65: 5, 'O God of our salvation', which the Greek translation renders 'O God our Saviour'. We should remember also that Jesus' name in Hebrew means 'the Lord saves', and this would be known to Aramaic-speaking Christians (see Matt. 1: 21). But the word was also freely used in pagan religion; for example, in the Mystery Religions the god was called Saviour as giver of new life and saving knowledge. These Mystery Religions were special forms of worship and belief that had grown up in the Greek-speaking world during the three centuries before the coming of Christ. They claimed to introduce their followers to a knowledge of God by revealing mysteries and initiating them into secret ceremonies. Perhaps the most significant use of the title Saviour, however, was in the worship of the Roman Emperor, who was called Saviour as the upholder of order and good government. It seems likely that those scholars are right who suggest that the author of the Pastorals deliberately uses the title (*a*) in rivalry with Emperor worship, and (*b*) as the equivalent for the Hebrew word 'Messiah' among Greek-speaking Christians. This would also apply to the author of 2 Peter.

Christ Jesus our hope. Compare Rom. 15: 13, 'may the God of hope fill you with all joy'; Col. 1: 27, 'Christ in you, the hope of a glory to come'.

2. *Grace, mercy, and peace.* Paul uses 'peace and mercy' in Gal. 6: 16, and 'Grace and peace' in Rom. 1: 7. The combination of all three occurs only here, in 2 Tim. 1: 2, and in 2 John 3. ✻

THE NEED TO OPPOSE FALSE TEACHERS

3 When I was starting for Macedonia, I urged you to stay on at Ephesus. You were to command certain persons to
4 give up teaching erroneous doctrines and studying those interminable myths and genealogies, which issue in mere speculation and cannot make known God's plan for us, which works through faith.

5 The aim and object of this command is the love which springs from a clean heart, from a good conscience, and
6 from faith that is genuine. Through falling short of these, some people have gone astray into a wilderness of words.
7 They set out to be teachers of the moral law, without understanding either the words they use or the subjects about which they are so dogmatic.

8 We all know that the law is an excellent thing, provided
9 we treat it as law, recognizing that it is not aimed at good citizens, but at the lawless and unruly, the impious and sinful, the irreligious and worldly; at parricides and matri-
10 cides, murderers and fornicators, perverts, kidnappers, liars, perjurers—in fact all whose behaviour flouts the
11 wholesome teaching which conforms with the gospel entrusted to me, the gospel which tells of the glory of God in his eternal felicity.

✻ At once the author launches into his main theme, a warning against the false teaching that was troubling the Church in his day and his region, probably Asia Minor. In this section he comes as near as he ever does to an attempted answer to the teaching. He says in effect that this teaching can only have a bad influence on Christian conduct and does not help Christian faith.

3. *teaching erroneous doctrines.* The English represents only one verb in Greek, a verb never encountered in surviving Greek literature up to this time. It may very well have been coined by the author. Ignatius of Antioch (died about 110–15) uses it. Ignatius may indeed be quoting from this passage, but we can hardly use this as a proof that Ignatius knew the Pastorals.

4. *those interminable myths and genealogies.* Outside the Pastorals, *myth* is only used once in the New Testament, in 2 Pet. 1: 16. The word would seem to point to Gnosticism rather than to Judaism. Gnostic systems of thought relied very much on myths; there was, for example, the myth of the divine being who descended into this lower world in order to rescue those men who had the divine spark in them. Philo, a learned Jew of Alexandria who died about A.D. 50, tried to combine Judaism and Greek thought, and he contrasts the Old Testament, based on history, with the pagan religions, founded on myths. On the other hand 'Jewish myths' in Titus 1: 14 shows that the word could be used of Judaistic teaching Moreover, *genealogies* suggests Judaism; the word could be used to describe the stories of the patriarchs in Genesis. And a Jewish book written about 135–105 B.C. called 'The Book of Jubilees' provides us with many examples of genealogies of biblical characters. The word translated *mere speculations* (one word in Greek) could mean a Jewish 'midrash'. A midrash was an elaboration of some biblical incident or passage, often supplying imaginary details which were lacking in the sacred text. The conclusion seems to be that the author of the Pastorals is facing a form (or forms) of teaching that combined both Gnostic and Jewish elements.

God's plan for us, which works through faith. The alternative translation given in the footnotes to the N.E.B. is worth noting: *the faithful discharge of God's stewardship*, but on the whole the translation in the text is to be preferred.

5. *this command.* Not the command of verse 3, which is a different word in Greek. Here it seems to mean the moral exhortation that goes with the proclamation of the Christian message.

from a clean heart, from a good conscience. The phrase *a clean heart* is used very frequently in *The Shepherd of Hermas*, a Christian book written in Rome probably at very much the same time as the Pastorals. *a good conscience*, familiar as the phrase is to us, is not found at all in the genuine letters of Paul. It occurs in 1 Pet. 3: 16, 21, and a similar phrase in Heb. 13: 18. The author of the Pastorals has a fondness for this sort of phrase. This suggests perhaps that he did not fully understand what Paul had to say about sin and faith.

7. *teachers of the moral law.* One word in Greek, found elsewhere only in Luke 5: 17; Acts 5: 34, where it means Jewish rabbis expert in expounding the Law of Moses. If this is the meaning here, then the author certainly has Jewish opponents in mind. The N.E.B. translation rather suggests 'experts in moral philosophy', who might just as well be pagan Gnostics. But on the whole it seems rather more likely that Jewish teachers are here in mind, though they might very well have constructed a Greek philosophical system based on the Jewish Scriptures, as Philo did.

without understanding either the words they use or the subjects about which they are so dogmatic. It is possible that we have here an echo of contemporary controversy between Christians and Jews. The Christian teacher would claim that he had in Christ a clue to the understanding of the Old Testament, hence the author's accusation against the teachers of the Law.

8. *the law is an excellent thing.* This is no doubt an echo of Rom. 7: 16, 'I agree with the law and hold it to be admirable' (same adjective in Greek as *excellent* here).

provided we treat it as law, literally 'use it lawfully', and 'lawfully' is a most unPauline word. The sense seems to be 'if you do not contravene the law, you can respect it and see its point. But if you break it, it is there to condemn you.' In Paul's writings the main function of the law is to show men up, to bring them to a realization of their impossible predicament. There is no hint of this in the Pastorals. In fact, according to Paul, you only realize that the law is *excellent* after you have broken it.

9. *good citizens*. A paraphrase rather than a translation. The Greek word means 'a righteous man'; the author then goes on to detail some of the sins of the unrighteous. Nothing could be further from Paul's teaching! See Rom. 3: 10, 'There is no just man, not one'.

the impious. Paul uses this word twice (Rom. 4: 5 and 5: 6). In the first of these two passages the phrase is translated '[God] who acquits the guilty', and the word for 'acquits' comes from the same root as 'good citizens' in verse 9 here. The author of the Pastorals could hardly say that God acquits the impious. In Rom. 5: 6, the N.E.B. translates the word 'wicked'.

10. *the wholesome teaching*. Notice that the behaviour which is condemned is opposed to *teaching*. Sin is thought of as transgressing a fixed law rather than as a broken relationship with a personal God. The author is very fond of that word *teaching*; he seems to indicate by it a fixed body of doctrine. Paul also uses it, in Rom. 12: 7 and 15: 4, for example. In the first of these places it probably means instruction for converts preparing for baptism. In the second passage it means information about Christ to be gleaned from study of the Old Testament. Here for the first time the word denotes a body of Christian doctrine.

11. *the gospel which tells of the glory of God in his eternal felicity*. As so often happens, the N.E.B. gives us a striking paraphrase rather than an exact rendering. More accurate would be 'the gospel of the glory of the blessed God'. It is quite possible that this means simply 'the gospel of Christ', for Christ is often presented in the New Testament as the glory of

God (compare John 1: 14; 2 Cor. 4: 4, 6). The phrase 'the blessed God' is much more reminiscent of Greek religion than Jewish. Nowhere else in the New Testament is this adjective used of God. The background of the author's thinking is Judaism influenced by late Greek thought and culture, technically described as Hellenistic Judaism. ✻

PAUL'S OWN EXPERIENCE AND
A BURST OF PRAISE

12 I thank him who has made me equal to the task, Christ Jesus our Lord; I thank him for judging me worthy of this
13 trust and appointing me to his service—although in the past I had met him with abuse and persecution and outrage. But because I acted ignorantly in unbelief I was
14 dealt with mercifully; the grace of our Lord was lavished upon me, with the faith and love which are ours in Christ Jesus.

15   Here are words you may trust, words that merit full acceptance: 'Christ Jesus came into the world to save
16 sinners'; and among them I stand first. But I was mercifully dealt with for this very purpose, that Jesus Christ might find in me the first occasion for displaying all his patience, and that I might be typical of all who were in
17 future to have faith in him and gain eternal life. Now to the King of all worlds, immortal, invisible, the only God, be honour and glory for ever and ever! Amen.

✻ In this passage we find the author at his best. He is dealing, not with theology or philosophy, but with the life and example of the great apostle of the Greek-speaking world, and he drives home splendidly the message of God's love for all, displayed in Jesus Christ. We find echoes of Paul's phraseology scattered all through these verses: *who has made me equal to the task* recalls Phil. 4: 13 'through him who gives me power' (same verb in Greek). And *appointing me to his service* recalls 2 Cor. 5: 18–19: 'enlisted us in this service . . . entrusted us with the message', where 'service' and 'entrusted' are the same words in Greek as *service* and *appointed* here. The words *the grace of our Lord was lavished upon me* seem to echo 'grace immeasurably exceeded' of Rom. 5: 20. One might guess that the author was quoting Paul from memory.

13. *abuse and persecution and outrage.* This must refer to such passages as Acts 8: 3; 9: 1. Though it is true that the persecution of Christians is persecution of Christ (see Acts 9: 4–5), the Greek does not actually say so in this passage. Compare also Gal. 1: 13, 'how savagely I persecuted the church of God, and tried to destroy it'.

14. *with the faith and love which are ours in Christ Jesus.* These words are rather loosely tacked on to the sentence. One rather gains the impression that the author, having mentioned grace, thought he ought to bring in faith and love as well, since they were such very Pauline words.

15. *Here are words you may trust.* This is the first of the so-called 'faithful words' in the Pastorals, always translated as *words you may trust* in the N.E.B. (the Greek is literally 'faithful is the word'). The phrase occurs also in 1 Tim. 3: 1 (where the N.E.B. has a different reading in the text but reproduces this phrase in the footnote); 4: 9; 2 Tim. 2: 11; Titus 3: 8. It is not always as clear as it is here to what exactly the phrase refers. It seems likely that the author is quoting something when he uses this phrase, but there has been much discussion as to what sort of material he is quoting. Some of the faithful words sound like a statement of doctrine used for teaching purposes, or like a hymn. One could without much difficulty make this one scan as poetry in Greek. Others have compared Rev. 21: 5 and 22: 6, where certain words are commended as 'trustworthy and true', and have suggested that they are words of Jesus, or words of Christian prophets, handed down from mouth to mouth and only now written down. This

might be true of this utterance, *Christ Jesus came into the world to save sinners*; we find parallels to it in Mark 2: 17 and Luke 19: 10. But it would hardly apply to all the faithful words in the Pastorals. The most we can say with assurance is that the author uses the phrase in order to mark with emphatic approval some formula which he quotes.

16. *find in me the first occasion for displaying all his patience.* A very fine insight: it suggests that there are no limits to the patience of God displayed in Christ.

that I might be typical of all. The word translated *typical* means a summary or outline sketch. It is only used elsewhere in the New Testament in 2 Tim. 1: 13, where it means a summary of doctrine. A similar word is used in 2 Pet. 2: 6, where the N.E.B. translates it as 'an object-lesson'. But the word seems to convey more a pre-enactment or foreshadowing of what is to come. Paul was to be the first of many apparently hopeless cases who would find rehabilitation in Jesus.

17. *Now to the King of all worlds.* We are certainly dealing here with a set phrase used in worship. Such a phrase is often called 'a liturgical formula'. It reminds us of two similar formulae in the New Testament, Rom. 16: 25–7 and Jude 24–5. Both these share with this passage the phrase *the only God* and *for ever and ever! Amen.* It is interesting to observe that both these other passages may well belong to much the same period as the Pastorals: Rom. 16: 25–7 is missing or displaced in some manuscripts, which suggests very strongly that it is a later addition not belonging to the time of Paul. The letter of Jude is generally believed to date from the period A.D. 100–10. *the King of all worlds* is a Jewish phrase, used in Jewish worship. It is actually found in Tobit 13: 11 in the Apocrypha. It also occurs in Clement's letter to the Corinthians, chapter 61, which was probably written in A.D. 96, before the Pastorals.

immortal, invisible. We naturally think of the first line of the well known hymn 'Immortal, invisible, God only wise'; but 'wise' is not part of the original text here. The two adjectives we do find in the text seem to echo Greek rather than Jewish thought. In Jewish thought God was invisible because it was dangerous to see him: 'man shall not see me and live' (Exod. 33: 20). In Greek thought he is invisible because he belongs to the realm of intellect and not of matter. From the occurrence of such formulae in the Pastorals and other documents of about the same date, we may well draw the conclusion that by the end of the first century the Christian Church was beginning to build up its own liturgies, using materials provided by the Jewish-Hellenistic religious tradition. ✻

A RENEWED CHARGE AGAINST
FALSE TEACHERS

This charge, son Timothy, I lay upon you, following that 18 prophetic utterance which first pointed you out to me. So fight gallantly, armed with faith and a good conscience. 19 It was through spurning conscience that certain persons made shipwreck of their faith, among them Hymenaeus 20 and Alexander, whom I consigned to Satan, in the hope that through this discipline they might learn not to be blasphemous.

✻ 18. *This charge.* It is not very clear what charge exactly, but it must be connected with the duty of opposing the false teaching.

that prophetic utterance which first pointed you out to me. We have no record in Acts or Paul's letters of any particular prophecy connected with Paul's choice of Timothy. The Greek is literally 'went before on you', so the phrase could refer, not to Paul's first choice of Timothy, but to Timothy's ordination by Paul. On the whole it seems more likely to have this meaning in view of 4: 14, 'the spiritual endowment you possess, which was given you, under the guidance of prophecy, through the laying on of . . . hands'. It is probable that in the author's time prophecy accompanied ordination. Christian prophets were very important people in the early Church. In the *Didache*, a Christian work which may not be very much later than the Pastorals, the Christian congregations have to be reminded that bishops and deacons are as important as prophets.

19. *So fight gallantly, armed with faith.* You will not find in the Greek any word corresponding to *armed*. The literal sense is 'by them fight the good fight'. Presumably 'them' means the prophecies.

20. *Hymenaeus and Alexander.* Hymenaeus is mentioned again in 2 Tim. 2: 17. Alexander is quite unknown. He is probably not to be identified with 'Alexander the coppersmith' of 2 Tim. 4: 14, who seems to be a non-Christian. Were these two actual contemporaries of Paul or of the author? They must be real historical characters, for there seems no reason at all why the author should invent two names of imaginary false teachers when he had plenty of real ones to pick from. It seems more likely that they were opponents of the author than of Paul. If we regard this passage as not being from Paul's pen, we must assume that the author is warning his readers against contemporary dangers. Perhaps the author wants to suggest that Paul had prophetically condemned these two, even though they could hardly be aware of it themselves some forty years before the date of its publication. A slightly similar situation occurs in 1 Cor. 5: 1–5, where Paul writes that he has disciplined a member of the Corinthian Church even though Paul was not in Corinth at the time.

whom I consigned to Satan. This is certainly an echo of 1 Cor. 5: 5, where Paul writes of the offender, 'this man is to be consigned to Satan'. The idea probably comes from Job 2: 6. God 'consigns' Job to the devil (same word in the Greek translation of the Old Testament) for testing. This would probably mean excommunication in the case of Hymenaeus and Alexander; but notice that it is not regarded as a permanent condition. The idea is that, the divine protection having been withdrawn, the excommunicated persons will be open to the attacks of Satan. These may take the form of bodily illness, but probably not of death, for the passage in Job runs: 'Behold, he is in thine hand; only spare his life.' In the early Church, as in the Church in Asia and Africa today, a person could be readmitted to communion after excommunication if he showed adequate proof of repentance and amendment. For *Satan* see the note on 3 : 6.   ✱

DIRECTIONS FOR PUBLIC PRAYER AND ABOUT THE PLACE WOMEN SHOULD HOLD IN THE CHURCH: 2: 1–15

✱ One scholar calls this chapter 'the earliest manual of church order we possess'. The author's rules are very general and seem to be dictated more by the pressures of his own situation than by any particular theory of worship. He wants prayer to be made for the Emperor because Christians are already being accused of anti-social behaviour by their pagan neighbours. He wants to emphasize the universality of God's call because the false teachers are suggesting that only the enlightened few can be saved; and he wants to keep the women in order because prophetesses are perhaps claiming undue attention and authority in the name of the Spirit.   ✱

PUBLIC PRAYER

First of all, then, I urge that petitions, prayers, intercessions, and thanksgivings be offered for all men; for sovereigns and all in high office, that we may lead a tranquil and quiet life in full observance of religion and high standards of morality. Such prayer is right, and approved by God our Saviour, whose will it is that all men should find salvation and come to know the truth. For there is **2**

2

3

4

5

one God, and also one mediator between God and men,
6 Christ Jesus, himself man, who sacrificed himself to win
freedom for all mankind, so providing, at the fitting time,
7 proof of the divine purpose; of this I was appointed herald
and apostle (this is no lie, but the truth), to instruct the
nations in the true faith.

8   It is my desire, therefore, that everywhere prayers be
said by the men of the congregation, who shall lift up
their hands with a pure intention, excluding angry or
quarrelsome thoughts.

✳ 1. *petitions, prayers, intercessions, and thanksgivings.* It is a
mistake to try to distinguish too clearly between these various
forms of worship. It is quite possible that the author is quoting
from a prayer himself. Verse 2 may also be a quotation from
a prayer. In Clement's letter to the Corinthians, chap. 60, we
have just such a prayer reproduced for us, including references
to the duty of obedience to the rulers, and a petition for a quiet
and orderly life for Christians. It is not surprising therefore
that Cranmer borrowed a phrase from verse 1 at the beginning
of the Prayer for the Church Militant in the Anglican Book
of Common Prayer: 'Almighty and everliving God, who by
thy holy apostle hast taught us to make prayers, and supplica-
tions, and to give thanks, for all men. . . .'

2. *for sovereigns and all in high office.* The author here touches
on an issue which is a live one in some parts of the world
today. In 1947, when India became independent, the question of whether the new rulers ought to be prayed for was
quite a burning one in the Indian Church. This was also an
issue in Japan just before the last war.

in full observance of religion and high standards of morality.
The two Greek words used here for *religion* and *morality* are
eusebeia and *semnotēs*, both favourite words with the author,
and neither found in the genuine letters of Paul. *eusebeia*
means 'piety'. It is interesting that the word occurs no less

32

than 47 times in 4 Maccabees, a Jewish sermon on the subject
of the men who died in the persecution of Antiochus Epiphanes in 170–164 B.C. It was probably composed about fifty
years before the Pastorals were written; as we shall be seeing,
this book, and the other Books of the Maccabees, were favourite reading with the author. It is impossible not to detect
a contrast between this ideal of quiet, pious citizenship and
Paul's picture of the strenuous Christian life (compare 2 Cor.
6: 3–10).

4. *whose will it is that all men should find salvation.* This was
probably written in opposition to Gnostics, who believed
that only an intellectual *élite* would find salvation; but in
later days it occasioned great difficulty for theologians who
held a strict doctrine of predestination. Augustine (died A.D.
430) explained it away as meaning that God willed every
variety of mankind to be represented among the elect, and
Calvin (died 1564) followed his example.

come to know the truth, literally 'come to the knowledge of
the truth'. The phrase 'knowledge of the truth' is almost a
technical term in the early Church for regular instruction
leading to baptism. It may even include the thought of baptism itself. In Heb. 10: 26 it seems to have this sense, as the
reference seems to be to post-baptismal sin: 'For if we persist
in sin after receiving the knowledge of the truth, no sacri-
fice for sin remains.' Compare also 2 Pet. 1: 2, 5–6. Most
scholars believe that these verses are a quotation from an early
creed. One scholar calls them 'a Christian version of the
Jewish *Sh^ema*''. The *Sh^ema*' is the great creed of Judaism, a
combination of Deut. 6: 4–9; 11: 13–21 and Num. 15: 37–41.
The first word is 'Hear!', for which the Hebrew is *Sh^ema*'.
It has been suggested that verses 5–6 are a quotation from the
long thanksgiving prayer in the eucharist (Holy Communion).

5. *one mediator between God and men, Christ Jesus, himself man.*
The word *mediator* is only used elsewhere in the New Testament in Gal. 3: 19–20 and three times in Hebrews. In Galatians it refers to Moses as the mediator of the old covenant on

Sinai, and in Hebrews to Jesus as the mediator of the new covenant. Nowhere else is Jesus called a mediator between God
and man. The word signifies an arbitrator who tries to bring
together two contending parties. This is the sense in which it
is used in the Greek translation of Job 9. The passage Job 9:
32–3 in the Septuagint (the Greek translation of the Old
Testament, henceforth referred to in this commentary by its
ideogram LXX) runs thus:

> For thou art not a man opposing me, to whom I might
> make answer, that we might come together to judge-
> ment.
> Would that there were a mediator with us to reprove us
> and hear thoroughly the issue between us.

It seems likely that the formula in 1 Tim. 2: 5 is based on this
passage in Job, and that this is where the phrase *himself man*
comes from. God has now granted to mankind the human
mediator for which Job prayed. If so, the formula is very un-
Pauline, for the mediator for whom Job prayed was to stand
outside both parties, being neither God nor man. Paul thinks
of Jesus as one who comes from the side of God to rescue
man, not as an arbitrator who mediates between the two.

6. *who sacrificed himself to win freedom for all mankind.* The
author is probably quoting a formula which is also reproduced
in Mark 10: 45, 'to surrender his life as a ransom for many'.
It is unlikely that he is consciously quoting Mark. Both passages go back to Isa. 53: 10, 'when thou shalt make his soul
an offering for sin'. In 4 Macc. 6: 29 a similar word to that
translated *sacrificed himself* is used to describe the death of the
martyrs.

proof of the divine purpose. The word translated *proof* here is
very frequent in the New Testament; on the whole the sense
is 'a fulfilment of God's promises in God's good time'. But
it can be used for bearing witness to the gospel, as in 2 Tim. 1:
8, where the N.E.B. translates it 'testimony'. Most scholars
incline here to the same sort of rendering as we have in the

text, but it could be taken to refer to the subject of the gospel preaching, in which case we must follow the R.S.V. in translating it 'the testimony to which was borne at the proper time'. This would give us a neat scheme: Jesus is the mediator prophesied in Job in Old Testament times, the redeemer who lived and died when God's plan came to maturity, the subject of the preaching now during the period of the Church.

7. *herald.* Used only here and 2 Tim. 1: 11 in the New Testament of the preachers of the gospel.

8. *by the men of the congregation.* In the author's time, as in Paul's, the leadership of worship was not confined to the authorized ministry.

lift up their hands with a pure intention. Clement in his letter to the Corinthians, chapter 29, has a very similar phrase: 'lifting up holy and unspotted hands to him [God]'. It is more likely that the author is quoting Clement than the other way round. Raising the hands was the gesture of prayer.

quarrelsome thoughts. This seems to combine two possible renderings. The text either means 'doubting, internal questioning' or 'disputes'. The former would be silent, the latter very much the reverse. Probably 'disputes' is the better rendering. Where worship is very congregational indeed, disputes are more likely to break out. ✳

THE POSITION OF WOMEN

Women again must dress in becoming manner, modestly 9
and soberly, not with elaborate hair-styles, not decked
out with gold or pearls, or expensive clothes, but with 10
good deeds, as befits women who claim to be religious.
A woman must be a learner, listening quietly and with 11
due submission. I do not permit a woman to be a 12
teacher, nor must woman domineer over man; she should
be quiet. For Adam was created first, and Eve after- 13
wards; and it was not Adam who was deceived; it was 14

the woman who, yielding to deception, fell into sin.
15 Yet she will be saved through motherhood—if only
women continue in faith, love, and holiness, with a sober
mind.

✻ 9. *Women again must dress in becoming manner.* This may well
have been part of the regular catechetical instruction (instruction for those preparing for baptism). We find a very similar
passage in 1 Pet. 3: 1–6. The tendency to keep women in the
background could be traced equally in the Jewish and the
Greek traditions. These seven verses constitute perhaps the
passage in the Pastorals which is farthest away from what we
are used to today. The author seems to be deliberately opposing what is generally regarded today as liberal and enlightened
opinion about women's place in society. Without in any way
assuming that Christians are bound to accept the author's
view because it is found in the Bible, we should all the same
bear in mind that our 'enlightened' view about women is
comparatively recent. Though we cannot go back to the old
ideal of women's status, the modern conventions which go-
vern women's place in society have still to be proved superior
to the old ones. We have not yet had time to see the full
effects of the change.

10. *women who claim to be religious.* This sounds self-
righteous, but the author only wants to distinguish Christians
from others.

11–15. At first sight these verses might seem to be fully in
line with Paul's teaching about women as found in 1 Cor. 11:
2–16; 14: 34–8; 2 Cor. 11: 3, and as reflected in Eph. 5: 22–3.
But a closer examination suggests that the author's teaching
here is different in a number of ways. In 1 Cor. 11: 2–16 the
man represents Christ and the woman the Church. This is
worked out more fully in Eph. 5: 22–3, where the conclusion
is certainly drawn that the woman must be subordinate to the
man, but only in the same way that the Church is subordinate
to Christ. That is, the relationship is one of love, not law, and

36

the purpose is the growth of both man and woman in close-
ness to God. In Eph. 5: 21 all Christians are urged to 'be
subject to one another out of reverence for Christ'. Again, it
is not by any means certain that Paul did forbid women to
speak in Church, as he appears to be doing in 1 Cor. 14: 34–8.
In some manuscripts there is a displacement of the text there,
so that verses 34–5 come after verse 40. This has suggested to
some scholars that these two verses were not written by Paul,
but were added later by some church leader who was being
troubled by obstreperous women in the congregation. The
new Peake's Commentary on the Bible (published in 1962)
actually accepts this view. Our author is apparently putting
forward the theory that women are inherently untrustworthy
as teachers because Eve, the common mother of all women,
was easily deceived by the serpent. Whether he also holds the
totally unPauline notion that women can redeem their unsatisfactory characters by bearing children, we will be con-
sidering below. At any rate it is clear that his teaching is not
by any means the same as Paul's.

13. *For Adam was created first.* The author probably means
that Adam was Eve's source, as she was created from his body.
There are traces of this idea in Paul (see 1 Cor. 11: 8–9). It
can also be found in Jewish writings of the same period.

14. *it was not Adam who was deceived.* The implication is
that Adam was not deceived by the serpent, but persuaded by
Eve. This view is not taken by Paul; see Rom. 7: 11, 'Sin
found its opportunity in the commandment, seduced me
[literally "deceived me"], and through the commandment
killed me'. Paul seems to represent himself as going through
the same experience as Adam, with 'sin' instead of the serpent.

15. *Yet she will be saved through motherhood.* If this translation is correct, it means that women, who inherit a peculiarly
weak and gullible nature, may yet be rescued by conscien-
tiously carrying out their true function, the bearing of children.
In Genesis 3 the pain of childbirth is the appointed penalty

for Eve's transgression. It must be confessed that this is
the most obvious interpretation of the phrase. But scholars
have naturally attempted to find some way of escaping the
conclusion that the author held so completely unPauline and
sub-Christian a doctrine. They have therefore suggested two
alternative translations. The first is 'saved through the Birth
of the Child'. This could mean that woman, condemned
because of Eve's transgression, will be saved through faith in
the incarnation of God in Christ. This would point in the
direction of that contrast between Eve and Mary that has been
a theme of Christian devotion all down the ages. Unfortu-
nately there is no indication in the text that this is what the
author had in mind. The third possible translation is 'brought
safely through childbirth'. This would make fair sense, if
taken with the next clause. Eve fell and was punished with the
pains and perils of childbirth; but women, her heirs, will be
safely brought through the ordeal if they continue steadfast
in the Christian life. But it is very doubtful if this meaning
can really be extracted from the Greek. A possible parallel
is found in I Cor. 3: 15, 'and yet he will escape with his life,
as one might from a fire'. One is tempted to prefer this last
translation, even if only for the sake of the author's reputation
as a Christian teacher.

if only women continue in faith. Here, too, is a difficulty: there
is no word in the Greek for *women*. Hence some have preferred to understand 'husband and wife' as the subject. The
reading in the N.E.B. footnotes is 'if only husband and wife
continue in mutual fidelity'. But this translation is incompatible with the third alternative translation of the previous
phrase (see above).

Just as the first half of this chapter showed us the author at
his best, so the second half seems to show him at his worst.
Christians are under no obligation to accept his teaching on
women.   ✳

QUALITIES NEEDED FOR THE CHRISTIAN
MINISTRY: 3: 1–13

THE BISHOP

There is a popular saying: 'To aspire to leadership is an **3**
honourable ambition.' Our leader, therefore, or bishop, 2
must be above reproach, faithful to his one wife, sober,
temperate, courteous, hospitable, and a good teacher;
he must not be given to drink, or a brawler, but of a 3
forbearing disposition, avoiding quarrels, and no lover of
money. He must be one who manages his own household 4
well and wins obedience from his children, and a man of
the highest principles. If a man does not know how to 5
control his own family, how can he look after a congregation of God's people? He must not be a convert newly 6
baptized, for fear the sin of conceit should bring upon him
a judgement contrived by the devil. He must moreover 7
have a good reputation with the non-Christian public, so
that he may not be exposed to scandal and get caught in
the devil's snare.

✻ The most remarkable feature of this list of qualities desirable
in a bishop is the fact that it seems to have very little connexion
with the actual duties peculiar to a bishop. The author is fond
of giving such lists; we find two more immediately following,
that for deacons and for their wives; and in Titus 1: 6–9 there
is a list of qualities desirable in presbyters. All these four lists
have much in common; indeed almost every quality requisite
for deacons is found in the list for a bishop; and if you take
away from the bishop's list the items found in any of the
other lists, you have almost nothing left. The only significant
qualities peculiar to a bishop are that he must not be a recent
convert, and that he must enjoy a good reputation with non-

Christians. Moreover, as we have already noted (see p. 16), the list of qualities needed for a bishop is very like a list of qualities necessary for a good general, compiled by a pagan writer. We may therefore guess that the author drew all his lists from some one list which may not have been originally of Christian composition at all.

1. *There is a popular saying.* The N.E.B. has here adopted the reading of some manuscripts, but gives in the footnotes the reading which is more commonly adopted by scholars: 'Here are words you may trust.' A few inferior manuscripts read *There is a popular saying* in 1: 15 also. This suggests that it is not original here, but was inserted in an attempt to avoid the use of the emphatic 'Here are words you may trust' in a context such as this, where there seems to be no very obvious saying worthy of emphasis. In fact so unremarkable is the *popular saying* here that some scholars, reading 'Here are words you may trust', would refer the saying to the last verse of the previous chapter. But 2: 15 fails just as much to supply us with a memorable utterance. The truth is probably that the author inserted this remark about trustworthy words more by way of indicating a change of subject than for any more complicated reason.

leadership, literally *episcopē* or 'oversight'.

2. *Our leader, therefore, or bishop.* There is only one noun in the Greek, *episkopos.* The N.E.B. is offering two alternative translations for one word. The word only occurs five times in the New Testament; besides here, Phil. 1: 1; Acts 20: 28; Titus 1: 7; and 1 Pet. 2: 25. In this last passage it is applied to Christ. In Philippians and Acts the 'bishops' can hardly be distinguished from the 'presbyters' in the local Church. Many scholars hold the view that those who were given pastoral oversight in the churches founded by Paul were called *episcopoi*, while the name 'presbyter' or elder was used for the same office in the mother Church at Jerusalem and in Churches dependent on it. During the period in which the Pastorals were written, the office of bishop as we know it today began

to emerge; that is, one of the *episcopoi-presbuteroi* began to be
given pre-eminence in each local Church, until by about A.D.
150 we find one bishop in each Church wherever there are
Christians. It seems very likely that the author was aware of
this development; it began apparently in Asia Minor and was
slower in reaching the West. In fact it is very doubtful if
there was any one bishop in Rome before about A.D. 120.
The fact that the author does not clearly distinguish between
the bishop and the presbyters probably indicates that he wanted
his words to apply both to churches where there was a
single bishop, and to churches where this office had not yet
emerged.

faithful to his one wife. This is one of five possible translations
for the Greek phrase in the text. The other four are as follows:
(*a*) 'married to one wife', (*b*) 'married only once', (*c*) 'married
not celibate', (*d*) 'not a *divorcé*' (alternatives (*a*) and (*b*) are
given in the N.E.B. footnotes). Of these five the most likely
are (*a*) and (*d*). 'married to one wife' is quite possible because
polygamy (a husband having more than one wife) was still
practised among Jews at this time, and the Church of the
author's day was still in close touch with Judaism. But on the
whole, 'not a *divorcé* who has remarried' is the more likely
in view of 5: 9, which is literally 'a woman of one husband'
(the N.E.B. there follows the same interpretation as it does
here). This must mean that she had not been divorced and
therefore changed her husband. It cannot mean that she could
have had more than one husband at the same time, since poly-
andry (a woman having more than one husband) was equally
foreign to Greek and Jewish ideas. On tombstones of the time
one often finds a woman praised for being 'of one husband',
meaning she had never been divorced. By analogy therefore
we apply the same interpretation here.

hospitable. We know from the *Didache* (see p. 30) that Christians were expected to entertain travelling prophets free of
charge. And compare Philem. 22.

4.   *a man of the highest principles.* This is that word *semnotēs*,

so much beloved of the author. It means little more than 'highly respectable'.

6. *a judgement contrived by the devil*. The alternative translation is given in the N.E.B. footnote, 'the judgement once passed on the devil'. This would imply that the bishop would be condemned for pride, as the devil was, and would constitute a reference to the old story, which we find occasionally referred to in the Old Testament, that the devil is a rebellious angel who was expelled from heaven for pride. But the next verse makes this unlikely, as *the devil's snare* is the snare contrived by the devil and not the snare into which the devil fell. The name 'devil' is originally a translation of the Hebrew *Sātān*. It originally meant simply an adversary, but long before the author's time it had acquired the meaning 'the evil angel, the tempter' and had been identified with the serpent in Eden. Paul always prefers the transliteration Satan (assuming that Ephesians is not by Paul), and indeed our author uses 'Satan' also, as we have seen in 1: 20.   ✻

DEACONS AND THEIR WIVES

8 Deacons, likewise, must be men of high principle, not indulging in double talk, given neither to excessive drink-
9 ing nor to money-grubbing. They must be men who combine a clear conscience with a firm hold on the deep
10 truths of our faith. No less than bishops, they must first undergo a scrutiny, and if there is no mark against them,
11 they may serve. Their wives, equally, must be women of high principle, who will not talk scandal, sober and trust-
12 worthy in every way. A deacon must be faithful to his one wife, and good at managing his children and his own
13 household. For deacons with a good record of service may claim a high standing and the right to speak openly on matters of the Christian faith.

✳ 8. *men of high principle*, the author's favourite word *semnos*. See the note on 3: 4.

indulging in double talk. The word is not met with in Greek literature before this; it might possibly mean 'wind-bags', but compare James 1: 8 'double-minded', a similar word.

9. *a firm hold on the deep truths of our faith.* Once more we find the N.E.B. offering a paraphrase. The Greek is literally 'having the mystery of faith in a clear conscience'. That word 'mystery' is much used in the New Testament. In the Gospels it means the inner significance of Jesus' person, which is hidden in the parables and can only be known by faith (see Mark 4: 11, where 'secret' is literally 'mystery'). In Paul it usually means 'God's mysterious plan, now revealed in Christ', but still only revealed to those who have faith; see 1 Cor. 2: 7, where 'his secret purpose' seems to be the translation of 'mystery'. In Revelation it usually means 'symbol'; see Rev. 1: 20, where 'secret meaning' is the N.E.B. rendering of the word 'mystery'. But the usage here is probably inspired by 1 Cor. 4: 1, where Paul describes himself and his fellow-workers as 'stewards of the secrets (literally "mysteries") of God'. So the word here probably means not only the Christian faith itself which the deacons are to preserve intact, but also the Christian sacraments, baptism and specially the eucharist, in which in early times deacons played a prominent part.

10. *No less than bishops, they must. . . .* It is not necessarily implied in the Greek that bishops must be tested before appointment.

11. *Their wives.* Many editors understand this in the sense of the N.E.B. footnote 'Deaconesses'. But 5: 9–16 seems to suggest that deaconesses were recruited from the ranks of widows, so the translation in the text is to be preferred.

12. *faithful to his one wife.* See note on verse 2. We would prefer to translate it 'not a *divorcé*'. This verse merely recapitulates the description of the ideal bishop in verses 2 and 4.

13. *may claim a high standing*. The phrase is a strange one in the Greek. With whom is their standing high? Probably with their fellow-Christians, though the idea of the approbation of God can hardly be left out.

the right to speak openly. This paraphrase conceals a Greek word meaning 'confidence' which is much used in the New Testament. It does not necessarily imply confidence in speech; compare Heb. 10: 19, which we may translate literally 'Having therefore confidence, brothers, to enter into the sanctuary'. It refers to the confidence of the Christian, who knows that he is a forgiven sinner. But, in view of Eph. 6: 19, it seems very likely that we should take it here to mean that the deacon of good standing will have confidence in speaking about the Christian faith. Eph. 6: 19 runs, 'and pray for me, that I may be granted the right words when I open my mouth, and may boldly and freely (literally "confidently") make known his hidden purpose (literally "the mystery of the gospel")'. ✻

QUOTATIONS FROM THE CHURCH'S WORSHIP

14 I am hoping to come to you before long, but I write this
15 in case I am delayed, to let you know how men ought to conduct themselves in God's household, that is, the church of the living God, the pillar and bulwark of the truth.
16 And great beyond all question is the mystery of our religion:

'He who was manifested in the body,
vindicated in the spirit,
seen by angels;
who was proclaimed among the nations,
believed in throughout the world,
glorified in high heaven.'

✲ The language in this short section is so peculiar that all scholars agree we have here at least one quotation from a Christian hymn (verse 16). Many think that verse 15 also contains phrases from the liturgy. One of the most interesting features of the Pastorals is the frequent quotation of extracts from contemporary worship. It gives us a much richer notion of what worship was like in this early period than we would otherwise have gained.

14. *I am hoping to come to you before long.* At first glance this looks like a piece of genuine Pauline writing, but a deeper consideration suggests that Paul would hardly have left Timothy so ill-trained that he would not know how to conduct himself in the local Church. The verse is therefore more likely to be an introduction to the sentence which follows, a convenient link between one piece of material and another.

15. *God's household.* In John 2: 13–22 it is hinted that the real house of God is Jesus himself; in 1 Cor. 6: 19 Paul describes the Christian's body as 'a shrine of the indwelling Holy Spirit'; in Eph. 2: 19–22 the whole Church is described as a building of which Christ is the foundation-stone. In 1 Pet. 2: 4–5 Christians are called 'living stones' in a 'spiritual temple', and in 1 Pet. 4: 17 the Church is called 'God's own household'. Both in that last passage and here it is possible that the right translation is 'house' rather than 'household'. Compare also Heb. 3: 6, where probably the translation 'house' should be retained throughout. The metaphor of the Church as God's or Christ's house is therefore a very frequent one in the New Testament, and the figures of *pillar and bulwark* used later on in this verse point in the direction of translating 'house' rather than *household* here.

the church of the living God. Curiously enough, this is not a phrase which is found anywhere else in the Bible. It may be an echo of Dan. 5: 23 in the LXX, where the Temple in Jerusalem is called 'the house of the living God'.

the pillar and bulwark of the truth. An unusual phrase; it seems to have been applied by the Jews, well after the time of the Pastorals, to the Great Sanhedrin, a college of scribes who made authoritative pronouncements about the interpretation of the Law; these rulings were widely accepted by orthodox Jews. But this title can hardly have been borrowed from the Pastorals, and we may guess that there is some common source farther back in time. *bulwark* is a strange word in Greek, never found in Greek literature before this. We cannot help suspecting some sort of a credal or liturgical formula. It would not be unfair to say that in Paul's writings *the truth* does not need a *pillar and bulwark*.

16. *And great beyond all question is the mystery of our religion.* This is not part of a formula, but an introduction to the hymn which follows. *beyond all question* represents one word in Greek, a rather unusual one, with an academic ring about it. It conveys the same feeling as would some such word as 'demonstrably', that is, it gives the impression of being a rather 'intellectual' sort of word. Why does the author use a word like this here? The answer seems to lie in 4 Maccabees, that late Jewish sermon which we referred to on page 33. This word 'demonstrably' occurs no less than three times in 4 Maccabees, in a sort of formula or refrain which runs: 'Reason guided by religion is demonstrably the right method of controlling the emotions' (4 Macc. 6: 31; 7: 16; 16: 1). It is in fact a sort of text for the sermon. 4 Maccabees is written in the style of a treatise on moral philosophy. We may suggest therefore that the author found this impressive-sounding word in his favourite book of philosophy, and adopted it in his own work in order to give an impression of learning.

He who was manifested in the body. . . . We have here, undoubtedly, a Christian hymn. In the N.E.B. it is divided into two verses, but we seem to get a better sense if we take it as three verses, each consisting of two contrasting lines. The contrast lies in the fact that one deals with Jesus in the earthly sphere, the other with Jesus in the heavenly (or spiritual) sphere. If we call the heavenly sphere A and the earthly B, we get the following scheme:

He was manifested in the body	B
vindicated in the spirit	A
seen by angels	A
proclaimed among the nations	B
believed in throughout the world	B
glorified in high heaven	A

He who was. The Greek is simply 'Who', and some manuscripts read instead 'God manifested in the flesh'. But *who* is no doubt the original reading. The very fact that it does not refer to anything immediately before it makes it all the more likely that it introduces a quotation.

manifested in the body, vindicated in the spirit. Compare 1 Pet. 3: 18, 'In the body he was put to death; in the spirit he was brought to life'. There too, no doubt, the same contrast of earthly and heavenly is intended.

seen by angels. This may refer to Christ's triumph over the unseen powers; compare 1 Cor. 2: 6–8, where Paul says that these powers failed to recognize Jesus as God; and 1 Pet. 3: 22, where the writer associates the subjection of all the powers of heaven with the resurrection of Jesus.   ✻

THE FIGHT AGAINST FALSE TEACHING: 4: 1–16

DESCRIPTION OF THE FALSE TEACHING

The Spirit says expressly that in after times some will **4** desert from the faith and give their minds to subversive doctrines inspired by devils, through the specious false- 2 hoods of men whose own conscience is branded with the devil's sign. They forbid marriage and inculcate absti- 3 nence from certain foods, though God created them to be enjoyed with thanksgiving by believers who have inward knowledge of the truth. For everything that God created 4 is good, and nothing is to be rejected when it is taken with

5 thanksgiving, since it is hallowed by God's own word and
by prayer.

* 1. *The Spirit says expressly.* . . . Where does the Spirit say
this? There are various references in the New Testament that
might illustrate this, such as Mark 13: 21–3 and Acts 20: 29–30.
But the author would certainly not have considered these
books as inspired scripture. It has been suggested therefore
that he had in mind some Jewish apocalyptic book which
has not survived. A better suggestion still is that he is referring
to the utterances of Christian prophets. We know that such
prophets played an important part in the Church of his day
(see note on 1: 18).

in after times. Probably the same as 'the last days' of which
we hear so much in the New Testament.

inspired by devils. Some elements in contemporary Judaism
were almost unhealthily preoccupied with the activities of
demons; e.g. the members of the Qumran Community,
judging by their writings as found in the Dead Sea Scrolls.
In the New Testament as a whole God's act of rescue in Christ
has banished the fear of demons, though there are references
to them as an accepted part of the religious background. See
2 Cor. 2: 11, where Paul is obviously not at all afraid of Satan;
compare also James 3: 15: worldly wisdom is described as
'demonic'. The Revelation of John is full of the activities of
the devil and his angels, who play the part of rivals to God
and Christ.

2. *the specious falsehoods of men.* Compare 1 John 4: 6, 'the
spirit of error'; Jude 18, 'men who pour scorn on religion',
and Rev. 16: 14, 'These spirits were devils, with power to
work miracles'. In all these writings, probably coming from
very much the same period as the Pastorals, we find the conviction that in the last days there will be deceivers and false
wonder-workers.

whose own conscience is branded with the devil's sign. This is
one possible translation of the Greek. It would mean that in

their heart of hearts they knew that they had sold themselves to the devil. The difficulty of this rendering is that the metaphor of *sign* or 'brand' is not very meaningful: what is the sign? A preferable translation is therefore 'whose conscience is hardened as if by a searing iron' (Knox). This would mean that they had lost all sense of right and wrong. Compare Eph. 4: 19, 'Dead to all feeling'.

3. *They forbid marriage and inculcate abstinence from certain foods*. This would seem to point to a form of Gnosticism. The belief that even marital intercourse is sinful is very common in nearly all forms of Gnosticism; for example, in the Gnostic 'Gospel of Thomas' the apostle Thomas is represented as going about persuading people to give up marriage. Something very like this belief took a firm hold on the Christian Church some two hundred years later; one of the most valuable elements in the Pastorals is this firm witness to the excellence of the married state. Indeed in this respect the author gives a more unambiguous witness to Christian truth than does his master Paul. The command to abstain from certain foods would remind us rather of Judaism; but this was also found in Gnosticism, and indeed there is no need to distinguish the two as far as concerns the false teaching encountered here. Compare Col. 2: 16, 'Allow no one therefore to take you to task about what you eat or drink'. Very much the same form of false teaching seems to have appeared in the Church in Colossae when Paul wrote his letter.

believers who have inward knowledge of the truth. The N.E.B. is translating a word which exactly corresponds to the word translated 'come to know' in 2: 4. There we suggested that the phrase implied regular instruction leading to baptism. No doubt the same is meant here. The initiated (i.e. baptized) enjoy full Christian liberty.

4. *thanksgiving*. Here, as in verse 3, the Greek word is *eucharistia*, the very word that Ignatius a very few years later uses for the eucharist or Holy Communion. It is very tempting to see an indirect reference here to the eucharist.

5. *since it is hallowed by God's own word and by prayer.* It is not at all clear what the author refers to. Scholars have three suggestions to make.

(*a*) The Word of God, Jesus Christ, has hallowed the creation by himself becoming part of it.

(*b*) The word is Gen. 1: 31, 'And God saw every thing that he had made, and, behold, it was very good'.

(*c*) The word is the blessing before meals, a custom which the Christians inherited from the Jews.

We may suggest a fourth:

(*d*) The word is the prayer of thanksgiving in the eucharist (this is not incompatible with (*c*)). Since God uses bread and wine for his purposes, nothing in his creation must be regarded as unclean in itself. We might compare an interesting passage in just such a thanksgiving prayer in the *Didache:*

Didache 10: 2–3	1 Tim. 4: 3–5
We *give thee thanks*, Holy Father, for thy holy Name which thou hast caused to dwell in our hearts, and for the *knowledge* and *faith* and immortality which thou hast made known to us through Jesus thy Servant. To thee be glory for ever. Thou, Sovereign almighty, hast *created* all things for the sake of thy Name, and hast given food and drink to men for their *enjoyment* that they may *give thanks* to thee; and to us thou hast granted spiritual food and drink and life eternal through thy Servant.	God *created* them to be *enjoyed* with *thanksgiving* by *believers* who have inward *knowledge* of the truth. For everything that God created is good, and nothing is to be rejected when it is taken with *thanksgiving*, since it is hallowed by God's own word and by prayer.

Identical or similar words in the Greek are printed in italics.

We may suggest that verse 5 corresponds to the explicit reference in the *Didache* to spiritual food and drink. The author would not wish to make a specific quotation from the central part of the eucharistic prayer, as this would be profaning the Christian mysteries. But it does seem likely that he is echoing an actual eucharistic prayer here.   ✶

HOW TO FIGHT THE FALSE TEACHING

By offering such advice as this to the brotherhood you 6 will prove a good servant of Christ Jesus, bred in the precepts of our faith and of the sound instruction which you have followed. Have nothing to do with those god- 7 less myths, fit only for old women. Keep yourself in training for the practice of religion. The training of the 8 body does bring limited benefit, but the benefits of religion are without limit, since it holds promise not only for this life but for the life to come. Here are words you 9 may trust, words that merit full acceptance: 'With this 10 before us we labour and struggle, because we have set our hope on the living God, who is the Saviour of all men'— the Saviour, above all, of believers.

✶ 6. *a good servant*. The word is *diakonos*, which in 3: 8 was translated 'deacon'. This shows that, though the word did indicate an office in the Church in the author's day, it could still be used in the more general sense of *servant* as in Paul's day.

sound instruction. The word for *instruction* occurs fifteen times in the Pastorals. It is found in Paul's letters (see Rom. 12: 7; 15: 4). But the author uses it for a specific body of doctrine which constitutes the Christian faith. This is not really what Paul means by the word.

7. *those godless myths*. *godless* is an unfortunate translation.

What we know about the Gnostic myths at any rate suggests that they were only too full of gods. If the author is referring to Jewish legends, then the word would signify that these stories 'had no real religious value', as one scholar puts it. The fact that the author adds *fit only for old women* (five words in English for one in Greek) would point in the direction of Jewish legends rather than Gnostic speculations, for Gnostic myths would probably be too highbrow for old women.

9. *Here are words you may trust:* the third of the 'faithful words'. The reading in the footnote in the N.E.B. shows that here too, as in 3: 1, there is considerable doubt as to whether the 'faithful word' refers to what follows or to what has just gone before. The translation in the N.E.B. footnote reads: 'The training of the body does bring limited benefit, but the benefits of religion are without limit, since "It holds promise not only for this life but for the life to come". These are words you may trust, words that merit full acceptance. For this is the aim of all our labour and struggle, since. . . .' The majority of scholars prefer in this passage to regard what has gone before as the 'faithful word', because the words that follow do not look like the sort of statement which we would expect to follow this formula. Thus the translation in the footnote seems the more accurate. At the same time it must be admitted that verse 8 does not sound like a particularly memorable sentence either. But at least it has the form of a maxim or general statement, which is more than can be said of verse 10.

10. This may well be a quotation from a hymn, for *With this before us* does not seem to refer to anything that has gone before.

the Saviour, above all, of believers. The author is striving against the Gnostic doctrine that God was only interested in the intellectual *élite*, but he also wishes to retain the Christian insistence that salvation was only for those who believe. It may be that this clause was added to the original quotation by the author. ✳

DIRECTIONS FOR RULING THE CHURCH: 4: 11 — 6: 2

✳ This section contains miscellaneous advice as to how various classes of Christians should behave, Timothy himself (who probably stands here for the bishop), the other ministers, widows, slaves. Whereas the last chapter dealt mainly with false teaching, this one deals with the other great theme of this letter, church order. The advice seems to be given more or less at random. Some people suggest that what was originally a very simple set of instructions has been added to in course of time before it was used by this author. Hence the disorder. ✳

TIMOTHY'S OWN CONDUCT

Pass on these orders and these teachings. Let no one slight 11,12 you because you are young, but make yourself an example to believers in speech and behaviour, in love, fidelity, and purity. Until I arrive devote your attention to the 13 public reading of the scriptures, to exhortation, and to teaching. Do not neglect the spiritual endowment you 14 possess, which was given you, under the guidance of prophecy, through the laying on of the hands of the elders as a body.

Make these matters your business and your absorbing 15 interest, so that your progress may be plain to all. Per- 16 severe in them, keeping close watch on yourself and your teaching; by doing so you will further the salvation of yourself and your hearers.

Never be harsh with an elder; appeal to him as if he 5 were your father. Treat the younger men as brothers, the 2 older women as mothers, and the younger as your sisters, in all purity.

✳ 12. *Let no one slight you because you are young.* This echoes
1 Cor. 16: 10, 'If Timothy comes, see that you put him at his
ease; for it is the Lord's work that he is engaged upon, as I
am myself; so no one must slight him'. But, if the letter
really had been written by Paul towards the end of his life,
Timothy would no longer have been young; so it looks like
a detail inserted by the author to keep up the convention of
Pauline authorship. In one of Ignatius' letters, probably
written within ten years of this one, he warns the Church to
which he is writing not to despise their bishop because of his
youth.

13. In this verse we have three quite distinct activities of
the minister in the local Church: (1) *Reading of the scriptures*
in public worship—the first reference to this among Christians. The scriptures would of course be the Old Testament.
(2) *Exhortation*, which no doubt included exposition of the
scriptures in the course of worship. The author of the letter to
Hebrews describes his letter as 'this exhortation' (Heb. 13:
22), and it is full of Old Testament exposition. (3) *Teaching*,
which probably means catechesis, i.e. the preparation of converts for baptism.

14. *Do not neglect the spiritual endowment you possess.* The
word for *spiritual endowment* is *charisma*, a word which Paul
uses for the various talents or abilities which God has given to
all Christians; see Rom. 12: 6–8, where 'gift' is *charisma*. In
this passage the *charisma* is connected with ordination. Some
scholars believe that this marks a deterioration in Christian
community life: in Paul's day every Christian might exercise
his *charisma* as best suited the needs of the Church; in our
author's day the *charisma* had been restricted to the ordained
ministry. But this represents a misunderstanding of both
Paul and the author: up to a period considerably later than
that of the Pastorals, there was no strict co-relation between
charisma and ministry. Ordained and unordained persons
might have *charismata* for various purposes.

under the guidance of prophecy. We have already noticed the

important place which Christian prophets hold in the life of
the Church. Obviously they had a part in the ordination of
men to the ministry (see note on 1: 18).

through the laying on of the hands of the elders as a body. This has
caused much discussion, because it seems to be inconsistent
with 2 Tim. 1: 6, 'through the laying on of my hands'. It is
possible to avoid the inconsistency by taking the one word in
Greek translated as *the elders as a body* to mean not a group of
people, but the office of presbyter. This translation is given in
the N.E.B. footnote 'your ordination as an elder'. This interpretation has been defended on the grounds that in Judaism
after the fall of Jerusalem in A.D. 70 there was a rite known as
'the laying on of hands to the eldership', which meant ordination to the office of rabbi. But even more relevant evidence
is supplied by the fact that Ignatius in his letters frequently uses
this very word *presbuterion* to mean the body of presbyters in
each local Church. It is very difficult to believe that the word
does not have the same meaning in the Pastorals, written, as
in all probability they were, at much the same period as
Ignatius' letters, and in very much the same area too. The
author is here witnessing to the practice current in his day:
the group of local elders consecrated the bishop by laying
on their hands. In 2 Tim. 1: 6 the author is referring
to the actual historical event of Timothy's ordination by
Paul.

5: 1. *an elder*. The word could mean merely 'an elderly
man', and the parallel with *older women* in verse 2 (which
certainly does not mean 'women elders') rather points this
way. We seem to find instructions for the discipline of ordained elders rather in verses 19–20. There is a touch of true
primitive Christianity in the exhortation to treat all Christians
as older or younger members of the same family. Compare
Rom. 16: 13, 'Give my greetings to Rufus, an outstanding
follower of the Lord, and to his mother, whom I call mother
too'. But similar sentiments are found in contemporary
pagan life; an inscription of the first century A.D. describes a

man as 'always honouring elderly men as if they were his parents, treating his contemporaries as brothers, and the younger men like his sons'. ✳

WIDOWS

3 The status of widow is to be granted only to widows who
4 are such in the full sense. But if a widow has children or grandchildren, then they should learn as their first duty to show loyalty to the family and to repay what they owe to their parents and grandparents; for this God approves.
5 A widow, however, in the full sense, one who is alone in the world, has all her hope set on God, and regularly attends the meetings for prayer and worship night and
6 day. But a widow given over to self-indulgence is as
7 good as dead. Add these orders to the rest, so that the
8 widows may be above reproach. But if anyone does not make provision for his relations, and especially for members of his own household, he has denied the faith and is worse than an unbeliever.

9 A widow should not be put on the roll under sixty years of age. She must have been faithful in marriage to one
10 man, and must produce evidence of good deeds performed, showing whether she has had the care of children, or given hospitality, or washed the feet of God's people, or supported those in distress—in short, whether she has taken every opportunity of doing good.

11 Younger widows may not be placed on the roll. For when their passions draw them away from Christ, they
12 hanker after marriage and stand condemned for breaking
13 their troth with him. Moreover, in going round from house to house they learn to be idle, and worse than idle,

gossips and busybodies, speaking of things better left unspoken. It is my wish, therefore, that young widows shall 14
marry again, have children, and preside over a home;
then they will give no opponent occasion for slander. For 15
there have in fact been widows who have taken the wrong
turning and gone to the devil.

If a Christian man or woman has widows in the 16
family, he must support them himself; the congregation
must be relieved of the burden, so that it may be free to
support those who are widows in the full sense of the
term.

✶ There was no state welfare system in the author's day, and
even charity was not organized on the scale that it was in
Britain in the days before the welfare state. Consequently
there was always a considerable number of people who were
really destitute: they could not earn their own living and they
had no one to support them. Of these, of course, the widows
formed the largest number, for the jobs open to women were
few indeed. The Christian Church, probably from the first,
undertook to support such widows among its own members
(see Acts 6: 1 and 9: 39). But by the author's time there seems
to have been a further development: an Order of widows had
been formed for those of them who were able-bodied and
devout. Apparently their job was to pray and to attend
Christian worship, and to carry out any subordinate tasks
that were given them. There is clear evidence for such an
Order in later times. In the Pastorals we seem to trace a vow
of celibacy associated with membership of the Order. The
widows in return were promised support for life. But all
destitute Christian widows seem to have been able to claim
support, so perhaps there was a higher stipend attached to the
Order of widows, and certainly the Order was regarded with
great respect in the Christian community. As we read this
section we must try to distinguish what is said about the

support of Christian widows in general, and what is said about the special Order of widows.

3. *The status of widow is to be granted* . . . . This, apart from being a rather free rendering of the Greek, begs the question about the Order of widows. The Greek is literally: 'Honour those who are really widows.' The word 'Honour' may convey the meaning 'pay', as in verse 17 (see note there); but it does not seem likely that the author has the Order of widows in mind here, for in the next verse he directs that children, and not the Church, must support their widowed parents and grandparents. He still seems to be pre-occupied with the problem of deciding whether a widow who claimed support from the Church was really destitute.

5. *has all her hope set on God*. This is almost a technical term in the Old Testament for one who has taken refuge with God; compare Ps. 91: 2, 'My God, in whom I trust', where the LXX translates by using the same Greek phrase as we have here. It is also found in 1 Macc. 2: 61, a favourite book with the author, as we have seen. Perhaps we should translate it here: 'she has taken refuge with God'.

the meetings for prayer and worship night and day. Here is clear evidence of daily public worship in the Church; not of course in a church building, but in someone's house, which would be open to all Christians in the town.

6. *given over to self-indulgence*. This probably means one whose sexual behaviour is unsatisfactory, for it is hard to imagine any other form of self-indulgence open to those who are destitute.

8. *he has denied the faith*. Compare Rev. 2: 13, 'You did not deny your faith in me' and Rev. 3: 8, 'you . . . have not disowned my name' (same word in Greek). The author shows a certain Christian common sense here; neglecting the most elementary human duties is no less to be condemned than the renunciation of Christianity itself. The later Church should have taken this more to heart; the tendency was to put heresy above all other crimes in the scale of wickedness.

9. *put on the roll.* Here, no doubt, we are to think of the Order of widows.

faithful in marriage to one man. On the analogy of 'a husband of one wife', we take this in the sense 'not a *divorcé*' (see notes on 3: 2, 12). The good works demanded of a widow must presumably have been done before she became a widow. If she was destitute she would hardly be in a position to do them.

10. *had the care of children*: not necessarily her own. She might have helped to look after orphans.

given hospitality, or washed the feet of God's people. This probably refers to the travelling prophets, who would look to the local Church to provide them with hospitality. In the East, where sandals are worn on bare feet and are taken off on entering a house, the first requirement for a new arrival is water to wash off the dust. Washing the feet of travellers is therefore not as elaborate an operation as it would be in the West. But it is a servant's job. In John 13: 2–11 Jesus washes the feet of his disciples as a sign that he has come to serve, not to domineer.

supported those in distress. The Greek word here is frequently used of people undergoing persecution; see 2 Thess. 1: 6–7, where it refers to persecution at the hands of fanatical Jews; and Heb. 11: 37, where it refers to the persecution of the Jews by King Antiochus Epiphanes in 170–164 B.C. But, as there is no other hint in the Pastorals of state persecution such as we find reflected in Revelation, the words here probably refer to any sort of distress, whether caused by adverse circumstances or by the unjust discrimination which any new aggressive minority group may encounter.

11. *Younger widows may not be placed on the roll.* There is no word for *the roll* in the Greek, but this is no doubt the correct interpretation. It looks as if a number of younger widows had impulsively taken the vow of celibacy required of those who were officially recognized as belonging to the Order of widows, and then shown by their behaviour that they were

unable to keep it. The author's remedy is to accept only elderly women into the order.

12. *stand condemned for breaking their troth with him.* The vow of celibacy was regarded as a sort of marriage with Christ. In much later times the woman who entered a religious order was called 'the spouse of Christ'.

13. *busybodies, speaking of things better left unspoken.* There is very probably a hint here of magical practices. The word translated *busybodies* is the same as that rendered 'magical spells' in Acts 19: 18. So *things better left unspoken* may mean charms and magical formulae.

14. *It is my wish, therefore, that young widows shall marry again.* To us it seems absurd that a church leader should direct people as to whether they are to marry again or not; but this is only because we live in a very different social system from that of New Testament times. In the social system of antiquity, a woman was not normally regarded as competent to manage her own affairs, and it was therefore considered perfectly reasonable that, among other important affairs, her marriage should be arranged for her. The woman herself did not normally resent this. Our modern system, whereby each woman is entirely free to arrange her own life, and especially her marriage, far from being the norm throughout history, is a convention that has only emerged in the course of the last century. It is not by any means accepted everywhere even today. In India, for instance, it is still very unusual for a woman to decide whom she is to marry. Such a choice is the privilege of highly educated women only.

15. *gone to the devil.* No doubt the true meaning of the Greek, which is literally 'turned aside after Satan'. It is probable that the *opponent* mentioned in the previous verse is also Satan.

16. *a Christian man or woman.* On the whole it seems more likely that the original text is better represented by the N.E.B. footnote 'If a Christian woman has widows in her family, she must support them herself'. It seems to mean that if a

Christian woman has the means to support the indigent females
in her family, she must do so and not expect the Church
to relieve her of the burden. We must remember that the
family would be a much bigger unit than what we are accus-
tomed to, including grandparents, uncles, cousins, etc. This
verse seems to have in mind the general support of the destitute, and not the special Order of widows.   ✶

THE SUPPORT AND DISCIPLINE OF PRESBYTERS

Elders who do well as leaders should be reckoned worthy 17
of a double stipend, in particular those who labour at
preaching and teaching. For Scripture says, 'A threshing 18
ox shall not be muzzled'; and besides, 'the workman
earns his pay'.

Do not entertain a charge against an elder unless it is 19
supported by two or three witnesses. Those who commit 20
sins you must expose publicly, to put fear into the others.
Before God and Christ Jesus and the angels who are his 21
chosen, I solemnly charge you, maintain these rules, and
never pre-judge the issue, but act with strict impartiality.
Do not be over-hasty in laying on hands in ordination, 22
or you may find yourself responsible for other people's
misdeeds; keep your own hands clean.

✶ 17. *Elders who do well as leaders.* There can be little doubt
that ordained presbyters are meant here. The phrase translated
do well as leaders is literally 'preside well', and this is a word
used some forty years later by Justin, a Christian writer
who lived in Rome. He uses it of the bishop presiding at the
eucharist. It is very likely that this function is implied here.

   worthy of a double stipend. We can hardly imagine that
Timothy, or anyone else, was in a position to double the
salary of a presbyter, quite apart from the jealousies which

would inevitably arise. So it probably refers, not to a regular salary, but to gifts presented from time to time to the presbyter or bishop by his congregation. At this time there must have been few Christians engaged as full-time church workers. Most presbyters would either have private means or some secular job.

those who labour at preaching and teaching. This suggests that there were some who did not. Perhaps we see here the emergence in each local Church of one presbyter with a gift for preaching and teaching who comes to be called the *episcopos.*

18. *For Scripture says . . . ..* This is quoted by Paul in 1 Cor. 9: 9, and may well be taken from there. The quotation comes originally from Deut. 25: 4, where it is a straightforward humanitarian direction. The other quotation comes from Jesus himself; it is found in Luke 10: 7. The author may be quoting Luke's Gospel as scripture; but it is more likely that he is quoting Jesus' saying as part of his oral tradition and loosely equating it with scripture.

19. *unless it is supported by two or three witnesses.* The author gives the Jewish practice as his authority (see Deut. 19: 15). Paul quotes the same passage in 2 Cor. 13: 1 in the course of his sharp dispute with the Corinthian Church, and Matt. 18: 16 shows that this was current practice in the Church where Matthew's Gospel was written (probably Antioch or somewhere in Palestine).

21. *Before God and Christ Jesus.* Why this solemn exhortation? Perhaps to impress 'Timothy' with the fact that he must judge impartially, since he himself will be judged after death. Notice that church discipline is carried out in public, as it continued to be for centuries.

the angels who are his chosen. A strange phrase, made stranger by the N.E.B.'s rendering of the Greek, which is literally 'elect angels'. We read of 'holy angels' in Rev. 14: 10, who are to witness the punishment of Satan. Compare also Rev. 3: 5, where the angels are among those who witness the final vindication of the faithful. The phrase here would suggest that there are also angels who are not elect, and so hint at a belief in the fall of the angels; but the author may not consciously have accepted this implication.

22.   *Do not be over-hasty in laying on hands in ordination.* The majority of scholars accept this rendering, but there is much to be said for the translation given in the N.E.B. footnote: 'Do not be over-hasty in restoring an offender by the laying on of hands.' In later times certainly one of the bishops' concerns was the readmission to communion of those who had been excommunicated but had shown genuine penitence; and this was done by a ceremony of laying on hands. Besides, this context would fit better with a piece of advice about discipline. A comparison with 2 John 10–11 also favours this interpretation. John is writing about a certain false teacher, and he says: 'do not welcome him into your house or give him a greeting; for anyone who gives him a greeting is an accomplice in his wicked deeds.' The Greek word represented by 'is an accomplice' is the same as that translated here as *find yourself responsible*. Another point is that it would be much easier to admit a person to communion in an over-hasty manner, as this would lie within the bishop's own discretion. To ordain someone would certainly require the consent, and probably the assistance, of the presbyters. This would be much more difficult to carry out hastily. ✻

DISCIPLINE OF ALL CHRISTIANS; THE RIGHT BEHAVIOUR FOR SLAVES

Stop drinking nothing but water; take a little wine for 23 your digestion, for your frequent ailments.

While there are people whose offences are so obvious 24 that they run before them into court, there are others whose offences have not yet overtaken them. Similarly, 25 good deeds are obvious, or even if they are not, they cannot be concealed for ever.

6   All who wear the yoke of slavery must count their own
masters worthy of all respect, so that the name of God and
2 the Christian teaching are not brought into disrepute. If
the masters are believers, the slaves must not respect them
any less for being their Christian brothers. Quite the
contrary; they must be all the better servants because those
who receive the benefit of their service are one with them
in faith and love.

✵ 23.   *Stop drinking nothing but water; take a little wine for your
digestion, for your frequent ailments.* The very ordinariness of this
advice would seem to be an argument for its genuineness. If
any verse in I Timothy comes from Paul's pen, this one does.
But it has not been included among the Pauline fragments
because it might have been written as a warning against
Gnostic food regulations. Just above the author has said:
keep your own hands clean. Perhaps 'clean' was a Gnostic watch-
word by which they advocated what we should call 'total
abstinence'. The author adds in effect 'I don't mean what
they mean by the word'. The Gnostics were opposed to the use
of wine because they were suspicious of anything that seemed
to indulge the body, reasons very different from those which
lie behind the modern movement for total abstinence, so the
advice given here cannot be taken as a condemnation of the
practice of total abstinence by Christians. On the other hand,
the sentiment here expressed is inconsistent with the opinion
of some fanatical advocates of total abstinence, that drinking
wine is altogether incompatible with true Christianity. The
decision for or against total abstinence today depends rather
on whether you think such passages as Romans, chapter 14,
and I Corinthians, chapter 8, apply to our modern situation.
In both these passages Paul suggests that things which are
quite harmless in themselves should in some circumstances be
avoided for the sake of weaker Christians.

24–5.   Compare with these two verses Rev. 14: 13, ' "Happy

are the dead who die in the faith of Christ! Henceforth", says
the Spirit, "they may rest from their labours; for they take with
them the record of their deeds"'. The two verses seem to be a
general reflexion on disciplinary experience. The reference to
court is a bit misleading to modern ears, for there is no question
of a law-court here. All disciplinary matters were decided by
Christians themselves.

6: 1–2.   In several other parts of the New Testament we find
advice for Christian slaves, though it is often coupled with
advice to slave owners; see 1 Pet. 2: 18–20 (advice to slaves
who have cruel and unreasonable masters), and Col. 3: 22 —
4: 1, with which should be taken Eph. 6: 5–9. In these last two
passages there is advice for slave owners also. Paul's letter to
Philemon gives us a valuable insight into the early Christian
attitude to slavery; it is summed up in Philem. 16, 'no longer
as a slave, but as more than a slave—as a dear brother'. See
also Titus 2: 9–10, where exactly the same advice is given to
slaves as here. And compare *Didache* 4: 11, 'Now you slaves,
be obedient to your masters with respect and fear as you would
to God'. Christianity is often criticized nowadays because it
did not from the first demand the abolition of slavery. But,
in the first place, this would have been useless; Christianity
had enough difficulties with the Roman authorities as it was
without adding to them by demanding a social revolution.
Secondly, early Christians expected the return of Jesus so soon
that the attempt to reform society would have seemed to them
hardly worth while. It can be honestly said that within the
Christian community the position of the slave was greatly
improved. By the year A.D. 220 a former slave, Callistus,
had risen to be bishop of Rome.

1.   *the Christian teaching*, apparently equated with Christianity.

2.   *those who receive the benefit of their service are one with them
in faith and love*. This represents a difficult phrase in the Greek.
It is not by any means clear that the Greek verb translated
receive the benefit of can bear this meaning, and the word

rendered *service* never seems to mean service rendered by an inferior to a superior. A possible alternative translation is this: 'they must be all the better servants because those who share with them in Christian service are one with them in faith and love'. This would mean taking *service* in the sense of *diakonia*, that lifelong service to which the Christian is committed by his discipleship to Christ. If so, the author is emphasizing the fine truth that both masters and slaves are really engaged in the same service, the service of men for Christ's sake. ✶

MISCELLANEOUS ADVICE: 6: 3–21

FALSE TEACHERS; THE DANGERS OF MATERIALISM

3 This is what you are to teach and preach. If anyone is teaching otherwise, and will not give his mind to wholesome precepts—I mean those of our Lord Jesus Christ—
4 and to good religious teaching, I call him a pompous ignoramus. He is morbidly keen on mere verbal questions and quibbles, which give rise to jealousy, quarrel-
5 ling, slander, base suspicions, and endless wrangles: all typical of men who have let their reasoning powers become atrophied and have lost grip of the truth. They
6 think religion should yield dividends; and of course religion does yield high dividends, but only to the man
7 whose resources are within him. We brought nothing into the world, because when we leave it we cannot take
8 anything with us either, but if we have food and covering
9 we may rest content. Those who want to be rich fall into temptations and snares and many foolish harmful desires
10 which plunge men into ruin and perdition. The love of money is the root of all evil things, and there are some who in reaching for it have wandered from the faith and spiked themselves on many thorny griefs.

✶ 2–3. *This is what you are to teach and preach.* One suspects that this is no more than a vague exhortation designed to hold together the miscellaneous material in this section rather than a request to pay attention to any particular piece of advice.

I mean those of our Lord Jesus Christ. He has not quoted any words of Jesus, so it seems likely that this is a reference to Christian teaching generally as originating from Jesus.

good religious teaching. His favourite word *eusebeia* recurs here, as it does in verses 5 and 6.

4. *a pompous ignoramus.* A neat rendering of the Greek. The author seems to have Gnostics in mind here, who indulged in the wildest speculations and most elaborate metaphysical systems.

He is morbidly keen, literally 'he is diseased concerning'. The idiom is found in contemporary literature: we read of one man who is 'mad on expensive jewels' and of another who is 'mad for publicity'.

quibbles. Both this word and the one for *endless wrangles* in verse 5 are unknown up to this point in Greek literature. Quite possibly they were coined by the author in his strenuous attempt to vilify the false teaching which was causing so much trouble.

5. *let their reasoning powers become atrophied.* This suggests an intellectual failure, but the author is probably thinking more of a moral defect. 'Whose mind has become corrupt' might convey the sense better.

They think religion should yield dividends. This suggests that the false teachers are making money out of their activities. Perhaps they offered a course of lectures and charged an entrance fee. It must be confessed that there have been many times in the history of the Church when the author's description of the false teachers would have fitted some of the orthodox Christians just as well. At such periods strict doctrinal orthodoxy, defined down to the last syllable, has been made a substitute for Christian life and love.

6. *the man whose resources are within him,* literally 'religion

with sufficiency'. The Greek word for 'sufficiency' is *autarkeia*, a key-word in the Stoic philosophy. Stoicism was a system of belief, amounting in many cases to a religion, which was popular among the educated classes in the Roman Empire. The word *autarkeia* describes a condition of inner calm, undisturbed by any outward circumstances whatever. A Latin poet has expressed it well in these terms: 'Though the universe may crash down upon him, he will remain unmoved among the ruins.' The passage that follows here is more Stoic than Christian in tone, and may have been taken from a collection of sayings about wealth which originally came from a Stoic source.

7. *because when we leave it.* The connexion of thought is not clear, so some scholars have suggested that the word for *because* was not in the original text and should be omitted.

9. *temptations.* The word in Greek, *peirasmos*, sounds like the word translated *dividends* in verses 5 and 6, *porismos*. There may be a deliberate pun, which we might render 'their receipts turn out to be merely deceits'.

desires. Another word very common in Stoic philosophy. Indeed this verse can be exactly paralleled in Seneca, a Roman philosopher of the Stoic school who had been put to death under Nero some forty years earlier. His brother Gallio is mentioned in Acts 18: 12 as the governor of the province of Achaia in Greece.

10. *The love of money is the root of all evil things.* This is a most unPauline sentiment. For Paul, the root of all evil was the rebellious will which turns away from God. See Romans, chapter 7.

there are some who. It looks very much as if the author had certain Christians in mind whom material prosperity had led to apostasy. It must be admitted that, despite the very obvious nature of the author's teaching here, it is remarkably appropriate to our day. ✶

A CHARGE TO TIMOTHY

But you, man of God, must shun all this, and pursue jus- 11
tice, piety, fidelity, love, fortitude, and gentleness. Run 12
the great race of faith and take hold of eternal life. For
to this you were called; and you confessed your faith
nobly before many witnesses. Now in the presence of 13
God, who gives life to all things, and of Jesus Christ, who
himself made the same noble confession and gave his
testimony to it before Pontius Pilate, I charge you to 14
obey your orders irreproachably and without fault until
our Lord Jesus Christ appears. That appearance God will 15
bring to pass in his own good time—God who in eternal
felicity alone holds sway. He is King of kings and Lord
of lords; he alone possesses immortality, dwelling in un- 16
approachable light. No man has ever seen or ever can
see him. To him be honour and might for ever! Amen.

* Many scholars believe that the author has incorporated into
this passage an excerpt from a baptismal address and perhaps
some quotations from a baptismal liturgy. The reference to a
confession and the formal phrases in verses 15–16 make this
conclusion very probable. Others suggest that what we have
here is rather a fragment of an ordination address; but there
is no evidence that at this period a confession of faith was
required from an ordinand.

11. *man of God.* This phrase is quite frequent in the Old
Testament; it is used of Moses, Samuel, David, Elijah, and
others. In the New Testament it is only found in the Pastorals;
but compare 2 Pet. 1: 21, where the last words of the verse in
Greek are literally 'men from God'. Behind the use of the
phrase here lies the thoroughly Pauline thought that all Christians are in the same relationship to God as were the most
favoured servants of God in the Old Testament.

pursue justice. This is not very like the way Paul writes. For Paul, righteousness (which the N.E.B. here translates *justice*) was not one virtue among many, but a description of the Christian's whole relationship with God; and anyway all good qualities were the gift of God rather than the object of men's pursuit.

12.   *Run the great race*. This seems to be inspired by I Cor. 9: 25–6.

you confessed your faith. Probably a reference to Timothy's baptism. The majority of baptisms at this period would be baptisms of adults, who could confess their faith themselves. This does not really conflict with 2 Tim. 3: 15 'from early childhood you have been familiar with the sacred writings', as if that phrase implies that Timothy had been a Christian from early childhood: the 'sacred writings' are the Old Testament, with which any devout and educated Jew would be familiar from early childhood.

13.   *Jesus Christ, who himself made the same noble confession.* There is an unexpected link here with John's Gospel, where Jesus is described as witnessing to the truth before Pilate; see John 18: 37, 'My task is to bear witness to the truth'. Indeed the parallel probably goes deeper, for the thought no doubt is that, as Jesus made his noble witness and then endured the Cross (which is called a baptism in Mark 10: 38), so the candidate for baptism first makes his confession and then undergoes baptism, which is itself a form of showing forth Jesus' death.

14.   *your orders*. Probably the baptismal vows. In the baptism service of the Anglican Prayer Book they are represented by the renunciation of the world, the flesh, and the devil.

until our Lord Jesus Christ appears, literally 'until the appearing of our Lord Jesus Christ'. The word for 'appearing' is *epiphaneia*; it was a word much used in the worship of the Emperor, and the author may be deliberately using it here in order to show that the true king is Christ, not Caesar.

15. *in his own good time.* Perhaps some Christians were claiming that they knew when the time would be (as they have done occasionally ever since). Or possibly some were saying that the time would never come. See 2 Pet. 3: 4: the author of 2 Peter had to deal with men who said, 'Where now is the promise of his coming?'

God who in eternal felicity alone holds sway, literally 'the blessed and only Dynast'. This is the only place in the New Testament where 'Dynast' is applied to God. But it is a most frequent title for God in the Books of the Maccabees, one more proof of the author's acquaintance with this literature.

King of kings and Lord of lords. Almost exactly the same title is applied to Christ in Rev. 17: 14; 19: 16. No doubt the motive is the same as here, opposition to the Roman cult of the Emperor as god.

16. *he alone possesses immortality.* The thought is Hebraic, for the Greeks on the whole tended to think that man's soul or mind was naturally immortal, while the Hebrews thought of life beyond death as always and only the gift of God. But the expression is Greek: there is no Hebrew word exactly corresponding to *immortality.*

dwelling in unapproachable light. Here also is a nice mixture of Hebrew and Greek belief. That God clothes himself in light, or builds his dwelling out of light, is a thought found in the Old Testament; compare Ps. 104: 2, 'Who coverest thyself with light as with a garment'. In Ezek. 1: 28 the prophet is overcome by the dazzling light in the midst of which God appears. But the addition *No man has ever seen or ever can see him* points rather in the direction of Greek thought. It was a strong tradition in Greek philosophy that God could not have anything to do with what was visible. God was therefore naturally incapable of being made visible. Both these strains of thought meet in the Fourth Gospel; see John 1: 18, 'No one has ever seen God; but God's only Son, he who is nearest to the Father's heart, he has made him known'. This is no doubt what is intended here, for we read in verse 15 that God will bring to pass the appearance of Jesus Christ, literally 'will manifest his epiphany'. Thus at two points in this short passage we have found a remarkable contact with the thought of John's Gospel. When we remember that Ephesus is very probably the place where that Gospel was written, and that most scholars date its writing at about A.D. 100, we realize that this connexion can hardly be accidental. ✻

A FRESH WARNING AGAINST MATERIALISM AND A FINAL WARNING AGAINST FALSE TEACHING

17 Instruct those who are rich in this world's goods not to be proud, and not to fix their hopes on so uncertain a thing as money, but upon God, who endows us richly with all
18 things to enjoy. Tell them to hoard a wealth of noble actions by doing good, to be ready to give away and to
19 share, and so acquire a treasure which will form a good foundation for the future. Thus they will grasp the life which is life indeed.

✻ Verses 17–19 resume the theme of verses 7–10. It is almost as if the charge to Timothy found in verses 11–16 was an insertion. But with a writer so lacking in the faculty of continuous argument as our author, attempts to rearrange his material are precarious.

17. *to enjoy.* This takes up the theme of 4: 3; the author no doubt has in mind the Gnostic teachers who condemned some foods as unclean.

18. *to hoard a wealth of noble actions.* The English suggests the thought of saving up a treasury of merit, which is not in the Greek. The R.S.V.'s translation 'to be rich in good deeds' is both simpler and more accurate. The author is echoing Rom. 12: 13–16, 'Contribute to the needs of God's people . . . Do not be haughty, but go about with humble folk'.

19. *and so acquire a treasure which will form a good foundation for the future.* The author is quoting the Book of Tobit 4: 9,

'For thou layest up a good treasure for thyself against the day of necessity'. Tobit is one of the books of the Apocrypha, written about 200 B.C. It would naturally go with the Books of the Maccabees, and thus form part of the Jewish literature which the author knows best. ✻

Timothy, keep safe that which has been entrusted to you. 20 Turn a deaf ear to empty and worldly chatter, and the contradictions of so-called 'knowledge', for many who 21 lay claim to it have shot far wide of the faith.
  Grace be with you all!

✻ Verses 20–1 add a further warning against false teaching, continuing the theme of verses 3–6.

  20. *that which has been entrusted to you:* only one word in Greek, 'the deposit'. It means no doubt 'the deposit of faith', the body of teaching which by the author's time had come to be regarded as constituting Christianity. This is not a Pauline idea but it does not deserve the condemnation which it has received from many scholars. Because we live in an age which is inclined to challenge and reject every form of tradition, we should be particularly careful not to ignore what is valuable in the idea of a deposit of faith. There is a tradition of Christian belief, thought, and practice which has to be handed on from generation to generation if Christianity is to survive. What is wrong is the suggestion that the tradition is sacred in the sense that it must not be scrutinized or criticized.

  the contradictions of so-called 'knowledge'. The word *contradictions* is literally 'antitheses', and this is the actual title which Marcion used for one of his books. Marcion was a Christian teacher who lived in Rome from about A.D. 140 to 160. He taught that the Old Testament did not reveal God at all, but that it was inspired by an inferior deity, who was the enemy of the true God. In order to discredit the Old Testament, he drew up a list of contradictions and inconsistencies in the character of God as depicted in various parts of the Old Testament. He was excommunicated as a heretic but founded a vigorous sect which survived long after his death. Some scholars have been so much impressed by the occurrence of this word *contradictions* here that they have located the writing of the Pastorals as late as 140, and claimed that they were written against Marcion. But, as we have seen, this view cannot be sustained. ✶

✶ ✶ ✶ ✶ ✶ ✶ ✶ ✶ ✶ ✶ ✶ ✶ ✶

THE SECOND LETTER TO TIMOTHY

CONTENTS OF 2 TIMOTHY

* Compared with 1 Timothy, 2 Timothy is less miscellaneous, and has a more unified theme, which might be called 'the life of the bishop'. Credal and liturgical matter is listed here in bold type, and genuine Pauline fragments or tradition in italics.

*   *   *   *   *   *   *   *   *   *   *   *   *

Character of a Christian Minister

ADDRESS

1 FROM PAUL, apostle of Jesus Christ by the will of God,
2 whose promise of life is fulfilled in Christ Jesus, to
Timothy his dear son.
Grace, mercy, and peace to you from God the Father
and our Lord Jesus Christ.

✡ 1. *whose promise of life is fulfilled.* This translates a vague phrase in the Greek, which is literally 'according to the promise of life which is in Christ Jesus'.

his dear son. Paul uses the adjective *dear* freely for his friends in the greetings in Romans, chapter 16. In 1 Cor. 4: 17 he calls Timothy 'a dear son to me', and he uses the same adjective of Epaphras in Col. 1: 7, and of Onesimus in Col. 4: 9 and Philem. 16. ✡

PAUL'S THANKSGIVING FOR TIMOTHY AND DESCRIPTION OF THE APOSTOLIC LIFE

3 I thank God—whom I, like my forefathers, worship
with a pure intention—when I mention you in my
4 prayers; this I do constantly night and day. And when I
remember the tears you shed, I long to see you again to
5 make my happiness complete. I am reminded of the
sincerity of your faith, a faith which was alive in Lois your
grandmother and Eunice your mother before you, and
which, I am confident, lives in you also.
6 That is why I now remind you to stir into flame the
gift of God which is within you through the laying on of
7 my hands. For the spirit that God gave us is no craven
spirit, but one to inspire strength, love, and self-discipline.

So never be ashamed of your testimony to our Lord, nor 8
of me his prisoner, but take your share of suffering for the
sake of the Gospel, in the strength that comes from God.
It is he who brought us salvation and called us to a dedi- 9
cated life, not for any merit of ours but of his own purpose and his own grace, which was granted to us in Christ
Jesus from all eternity, but has now at length been brought 10
fully into view by the appearance on earth of our Saviour
Jesus Christ. For he has broken the power of death and
brought life and immortality to light through the Gospel.

Of this Gospel I, by his appointment, am herald, 11
apostle, and teacher. That is the reason for my present 12
plight; but I am not ashamed of it, because I know who
it is in whom I have trusted, and am confident of his
power to keep safe what he has put into my charge, until
the great Day. Keep before you an outline of the sound 13
teaching which you heard from me, living by the faith
and love which are ours in Christ Jesus. Guard the trea- 14
sure put into our charge, with the help of the Holy
Spirit dwelling within us.

✻ The author imagines Paul as writing from prison not long
before his death. He gives a vivid and moving picture of the
strenuous and dangerous life of an apostle. We can compare
with this Paul's own words in 1 Cor. 4: 9–13 and 2 Cor. 6:
3–10. In both these passages the perils and labours are em-
phasized, but so is his complete reliance on God in Christ.

3. *whom I, like my forefathers, worship with a pure intention.*
The verse seems to be modelled on Rom. 1: 9, 'the God to
whom I offer the humble service of my spirit'. In Greek 'offer
the humble service' and *worship* are the same word. *forefathers*
may be an echo of Acts 24: 14 'it is in that manner that I worship the God of our fathers'. Or the author may be hinting

that Paul is as faithful to the God of his forefathers as is any orthodox Jew. The word rendered *intention* here is more often translated 'conscience'. The phrase 'a clear conscience' is characteristic of the author: Paul himself would hardly have claimed a clear conscience quite so easily or so often.

4. *the tears you shed*, probably at parting.

5. *Lois your grandmother and Eunice your mother*. This is undoubtedly an authentic piece of information about Timothy. But we must not indulge in too rosy a picture of Timothy's religious upbringing, for we are told in Acts 16: 1 that, though Timothy's mother was a Jewess converted to Christianity, his father was a Greek. This means that his mother by marrying a gentile automatically excommunicated herself from the orthodox Jewish community. We may reasonably suggest that Eunice became a Christian after her husband's death (a few manuscripts of Acts add the word 'widow' after 'Jewish' in Acts 16: 1); we may also guess that Lois was converted at the same time.

6. *the gift of God which is within you through the laying on of my hands*. See the note on 1 Tim. 4: 14, where it is claimed that this passage here witnesses to the way in which Timothy was actually ordained, and the passage in 1 Timothy to the ordination practice usual in the author's day.

7. *no craven spirit*. Perhaps it ought to be 'Spirit'; compare Rom. 8: 15, 'The Spirit you have received is not a spirit of slavery leading you back into a life of fear, but a Spirit that makes us sons'.

8. *your testimony to our Lord*. The Greek word for *testimony* is *marturion*, and there may be a hint of martyrdom here. We know that Timothy did actually suffer imprisonment (see Heb. 13: 23).

9. Several scholars think that this verse is in fact a quotation. It has been called 'a Christian hymn', 'a credal fragment', 'a preaching formula'. The thought is not very clear, for the purposed salvation can be said to have been in some sense *granted to us . . . from all eternity*, but hardly the grace.

78

10. This sounds very like a liturgical fragment. The *appearance on earth* is *epiphany* in Greek. With *he has broken the power of death* compare 1 Cor. 15: 26, 'the last enemy to be abolished (same word in Greek as *broken the power* here) is death'. An even closer parallel is Heb. 2: 14, 'through death he might break the power of him who had death at his command, that is, the devil'.

brought life and immortality to light. This strange phrase points to the liturgical language lying behind this passage. It may well be an extract from the Thanksgiving Prayer at the eucharist. In this prayer it would be quite appropriate to offer thanks to God for the two sacraments, baptism and the eucharist. We have quoted just such a prayer from the *Didache* in the note on 1 Tim. 4: 5. The word for *brought to light* is used by Justin (some fifty years later, perhaps) for baptism, and *immortality* may be an indirect reference to the eucharist. Ignatius called the eucharist 'a medicine of deathlessness, an antidote against dying'. The word *immortality* is used twice in the Book of Wisdom and three times in 4 Maccabees for life after death. If we adopt this interpretation we avoid the problem which has perplexed some scholars: does the passage suggest that life and immortality were waiting to be discovered by Christ? In fact the author only uses the verb as an indirect method of referring to baptism. To sum up: the author is varying his material by quoting from part of a Thanksgiving Prayer used at the eucharist in which God is praised for granting to us in Christ the gifts of both baptism and the eucharist.

11. *herald, apostle, and teacher.* Paul often uses the word 'to herald' of preaching the gospel, but never elsewhere calls himself a herald.

12. *what he has put into my charge.* As the reading in the footnotes in the N.E.B. indicates, this could just as well mean 'what I have put into his charge'. The older editors tend to prefer this rendering and interpret it of Paul's own soul. But, in view of the fact that the phrase translates the same

word in Greek as is translated *treasure put into our charge* in verse 14, it seems better to understand it of 'the deposit of faith', the substance of the gospel message. God will keep Paul faithful to that message.

13. *Keep before you an outline of the sound teaching*. This could be understood in two different ways: (*a*) as in the text here: in this case Timothy is being urged to keep in mind the main outline of the Christian tradition, but is not being reminded of any particular credal formula; (*b*) 'hold on to the pattern of sound words which you have heard from me'. In this case the author is commending a specific creed. The reading in the footnotes of the N.E.B. on the whole supports this interpretation, 'Keep before you as a model of sound teaching that which . . .'. But the Greek word translated *model* does not really admit this meaning. It means an outline, rough sketch, perhaps a blueprint. It is better therefore to stick to the N.E.B. text and to understand the author as commending adherence to the general Christian tradition.

14. *with the help of the Holy Spirit dwelling within us*. Here *the treasure* is the deposit of faith or sum of Christian teaching. Several scholars have drawn the conclusion from this that according to the author the ordained ministry was specially endowed with the Spirit for the purpose of teaching. This may well be the case, but it does not necessarily follow; it may be an echo of Rom. 8: 11, where the Spirit is understood as dwelling in all Christians; and in 2 Cor. 6: 16 and Col. 3: 16 God or Christ is described as dwelling in all Christians. *

A PAULINE FRAGMENT

15 As you know, everyone in the province of Asia de-
16 serted me, including Phygelus and Hermogenes. But may the Lord's mercy rest on the house of Onesiphorus! He has often relieved me in my troubles. He was not
17 ashamed to visit a prisoner, but took pains to search me

out when he came to Rome, and found me. I pray that the 18
Lord may grant him to find mercy from the Lord on the
great Day. The many services he rendered at Ephesus you
know better than I could tell you.

✻ The great majority of scholars agree that we have genuine
information about Paul in these verses. The only question is:
do the words come directly from Paul, or is the information
contained in words supplied by the author? It seems simpler
to assume that the words do come from Paul. There is nothing
(or almost nothing) unPauline in the passage.

15. *everyone in the province of Asia deserted me*. This must
refer to something that happened in Asia and not in Rome.
Timothy knows about it, so we must suppose that Paul was
arrested in Asia, and at his interrogation in the town where he
was arrested his friends, whom he had expected to support
him, failed to rally round.

16. *the house of Onesiphorus*. He must have been a native
of Asia, probably Ephesus; see 4: 19, which we take to be
genuinely Pauline material. Presumably he was in Rome on
business and took great pains to find out where Paul was im-
prisoned. Most scholars conclude that Onesiphorus was dead
by the time that this was written. Otherwise, they argue,
Paul would surely have referred to Onesiphorus himself as
well as to his household. If so, then Paul does actually pray
for one who is dead. But this can hardly be said to throw very
much light on what Paul thought about the condition of those
who have died as believers, for Paul probably expects the
great *Day* of final judgement to come very soon.

18. *I pray that the Lord may grant him to find mercy from the
Lord*. This is a most awkward expression and makes one
wonder whether this verse comes from Paul's pen. The first
Lord is no doubt God and the second Christ.

you know better than I could tell you. A more accurate translation might be 'you know very well'. ✻

ADVICE ON THE LIFE OF A BISHOP, WITH
SPECIAL REFERENCE TO THE DUTY OF OPPOSING
FALSE TEACHING: 2: 1–26

THE NEED FOR COURAGE

2 Now therefore, my son, take strength from the grace of
2 God which is ours in Christ Jesus. You heard my teaching
in the presence of many witnesses; put that teaching into
the charge of men you can trust, such men as will be
competent to teach others.

3   Take your share of hardship, like a good soldier of
4 Christ Jesus. A soldier on active service will not let himself be involved in civilian affairs; he must be wholly at
5 his commanding officer's disposal. Again, no athlete can
6 win a prize unless he has kept the rules. The farmer who
7 gives his labour has first claim on the crop. Reflect on
what I say, for the Lord will help you to full understanding.

✶ We now turn back again to the rather pedestrian exhortation of the author. He seems in this passage to be trying to
justify both the authority and the payment of the bishops of
his day.

2. *You heard my teaching in the presence of many witnesses.*
This does not sound like the real Paul writing to the real
Timothy. After several years of missionary work together,
the elder man is not likely to want to remind the other of the
teaching they are both imparting. It sounds more like a re-
minder to the Church in the author's day that traditional
Christian teaching could trace its lineage right back to Paul.
The reference to *witnesses* probably means baptism.

put that teaching into the charge of men you can trust. Here is
perhaps the nearest thing to the doctrine of the 'apostolic
succession' that we can find in the Bible. This is the theory

82

that Christ gave his authority to the apostles, that they
handed it on to the first bishops, and that it has descended by
succession of ordination to the bishops of today. There is an
earlier reference, but not in the New Testament. It occurs in
Clement's letter, chapters 42–4, where Clement says that the
apostles appointed their first converts to superintend the
congregations, and that they in their turn were succeeded
by 'approved men with the consent of the whole Church'.
Notice that in Timothy the succession is a succession in doctrine rather than in ordination. What the author is concerned
about is not that each bishop should have been succeeded by a
bishop properly ordained, but that each bishop should have
been succeeded by someone who maintained the same teaching as his predecessor. This is what the apostolic succession
meant in the second century A.D. It was only later that im-
portance came to be laid on succession in ordination. Whether
in fact Paul did formally hand down his teaching to chosen
men in each Church which he founded, we cannot say with
certainty. At any rate, whether formally conveyed or not,
enough of Paul's gospel was handed down to prevent the
Christian message being overwhelmed by the non-Christian
atmosphere that surrounded it.

4–5. The author uses three metaphors to help out his meaning, the soldier, the athlete, and the farmer. All are used by
Paul: for the metaphor of warfare, see 2 Cor. 10: 3–5; for
the athlete, see 1 Cor. 9: 25–7; for the farmer, see 1 Cor. 9:
7–10.

5. *can win a prize.* The N.E.B. has rightly rendered the
Greek into modern terms. It is literally 'can be crowned'.

unless he has kept the rules. Curiously enough, it may be the
rules of right training that are alluded to here rather than the
rules of the game.

7. This is almost a quotation from Paul, who writes in
1 Cor. 9: 7, 'Did you ever hear of a man serving in the army at
his own expense? or planting a vineyard without eating the
fruit of it? or tending a flock without using its milk?'

Reflect on what I say. On the face of it, this would seem a strange injunction, for the author has said nothing very profound or difficult to understand; but he is probably hinting that bishops have a right to some measure of support from their flocks. This is the argument from the passage in 1 Corinthians, chapter 9, to which he alludes. He is probably using indirect language because he knows the letter may be read out in Church, and he does not want to be too mercenary. Paul, in 2 Corinthians, chapters 8 and 9, shows a similar tendency to be allusive rather than direct when writing of the financial obligations of the Churches. ✶

A CREDAL INTERLUDE

8 Remember Jesus Christ, risen from the dead, born of
9 David's line. This is the theme of my gospel, in whose service I am exposed to hardship, even to the point of being shut up like a common criminal; but the word of
10 God is not shut up. And I endure it all for the sake of God's chosen ones, with this end in view, that they too may attain the glorious and eternal salvation which is in Christ Jesus.

11   Here are words you may trust:

      'If we died with him, we shall live with him;
12   If we endure, we shall reign with him.
       If we deny him, he will deny us.
13   If we are faithless, he keeps faith,
         For he cannot deny himself.'

✶ It seems possible that this section has been introduced primarily for the sake of the credal or liturgical material which it contains.

8. *risen from the dead, born of David's line.* This reminds one of Rom. 1: 3–4; see also the note on 1 Tim. 3: 16.

84

9. *even to the point of being shut up.* A frequent theme with Paul; see Phil. 1: 7–17; Philem. 9–13.

10. *for the sake of God's chosen ones.* This probably means simply 'my fellow-Christians', as in 1 Pet. 1: 1–2.

11. The fourth of the 'faithful words'. Here it is obvious what the formula refers to—the hymn or creed which follows. Nearly all scholars agree that it is a hymn, and most would connect it with a baptismal liturgy.

If we died with him. Probably a reference to baptism rather than martyrdom. We could compare 2 Cor. 4: 11, 'while still alive, we are being surrendered into the hands of death, for Jesus' sake'. But Paul is more profound there, for he is writing of the strenuous, dangerous life of the ministers, a 'death in life'. Here the hymn merely promises future life in return for the 'death' which baptism represents.

12. *we shall reign with him.* In the future life; in the New Testament reigning always takes place in the life to come, not in this life. See 1 Cor. 4: 8, 'You have come into your kingdom—and left us out'. The Corinthians' mistake was to imagine that they were reigning already.

If we deny him, he will deny us. This is expressed graphically in the parable of the sheep and the goats in Matt. 25: 31–46, and explicitly in Matt. 10: 33, 'whoever disowns me before men, I will disown him before my Father in heaven'.

13. Is this a threat or a promise? On the whole it seems better to follow those who take it as an encouraging promise. The author is no grim rigorist and always emphasizes the wideness of God's mercy. It seems likely that the last clause *For he cannot deny himself* is the author's own addition to the hymn: God's nature is to love and to save whatever can be saved, and to this he adheres even though men prove inconstant. ✳

GENERAL WARNINGS AGAINST FALSE TEACHING

14 Go on reminding people of this, and adjure them before God to stop disputing about mere words; it does no good,

15 and is the ruin of those who listen. Try hard to show yourself worthy of God's approval, as a labourer who need not be ashamed, driving a straight furrow, in your

16 proclamation of the truth. Avoid empty and worldly chatter; those who indulge in it will stray further and

17 further into godless courses, and the infection of their teaching will spread like a gangrene. Such are Hyme-

18 naeus and Philetus; they have shot wide of the truth in saying that our resurrection has already taken place, and

19 are upsetting people's faith. But God has laid a foundation, and it stands firm, with this inscription: 'The Lord knows his own', and, 'Everyone who takes the Lord's

20 name upon his lips must forsake wickedness.' Now in any great house there are not only utensils of gold and silver, but also others of wood or earthenware; the former are

21 valued, the latter held cheap. To be among those which are valued and dedicated, a thing of use to the Master of the house, a man must cleanse himself from all those evil things; then he will be fit for any honourable purpose.

22 Turn from the wayward impulses of youth, and pursue justice, integrity, love, and peace with all who invoke

23 the Lord in singleness of mind. Have nothing to do with foolish and ignorant speculations. You know they breed

24 quarrels, and the servant of the Lord must not be quarrelsome, but kindly towards all. He should be a good tea-

25 cher, tolerant, and gentle when discipline is needed for the refractory. The Lord may grant them a change of

heart and show them the truth, and thus they may come 26
to their senses and escape from the devil's snare, in which
they have been caught and held at his will.

✴ This is a most characteristic passage, joining together warnings against false teaching and descriptions of the ministerial
life, with an attempt to reproduce a metaphor used by Paul in
Romans. The whole is constructed on no clear system, but
seems to wander from one topic to another in a way not at all
reminiscent of Paul.

15.   *Try hard.* The author encourages strenuous moral effort
without asking the deeper questions that occupied Paul's
mind concerning the working of God's grace.

a labourer who need not be ashamed. More accurately, 'a
labourer who cannot be refuted'.

driving a straight furrow. The precise meaning of the Greek
here is not clear. It is literally 'rightly cutting the word of
truth'. 'The word of truth' is the gospel, and no doubt the
general meaning is 'correctly expounding the gospel, unlike
the false teachers who misrepresent it'; but whether the metaphor is taken from ploughing a straight furrow, hewing stones
exactly square, or driving a straight road through unoccupied
territory, is not clear.

16.   *will stray further and further,* literally 'progress'. Compare 2 John 9, 'Anyone who runs ahead too far . . . '. The
author had no sympathy with the 'progressive' party.

18.   *Hymenaeus and Philetus.* The first has been mentioned in
1 Tim. 1: 20. We suggested that he was probably a contemporary of the author.

saying that our resurrection has already taken place. We may
guess from this that they were Gnostics rather than Jewish
teachers. Jews would have demanded concrete evidence of
the resurrection, but the Christian doctrine of the resurrection of the body met with a natural resistance among Greek
thinkers, and the tendency would be to explain it away in purely
spiritual, intellectual, or mystical terms. Once this had been

done it would be easy to say that (spiritually, intellectually, or mystically) the resurrection had already taken place. We find the same teaching condemned in *The Acts of Paul*, an apocryphal book written in Asia Minor in the second century, and also in *The Second Letter of Clement*. This is a letter, mistakenly attributed to Clement, written about A.D. 160. Paul's teaching about the Christian life could easily lead to some such misunderstanding; see Col. 3: 1, 'Were you not raised to life with Christ?'

19. *God has laid a foundation* . . . . The foundation is presumably either the revelation of God in Jesus Christ or the traditional teaching that safeguards this.

inscription, literally 'seal'. It is easy to see why the author chooses the first of these two quotations. It comes from Num. 16: 5, and is uttered by Moses on the occasion of the revolt of Korah, Dathan, and Abiram against his authority. In the Old Testament story the rebels were ultimately swallowed up by the earth. No doubt the author wishes to suggest that the refractory teachers Hymenaeus and Philetus are in the same category and may share the same fate. There is a similar reference in Jude 11, 'they have rebelled like Korah, and they share his doom'. Indeed the author of Jude seems to be dealing with a very similar movement. The difficulty arises when we try to trace the source of the other quotation: it cannot be exactly found in the Old Testament. On the contrary, 'to name the name of the Lord' in the Old Testament properly means to utter the worst sort of blasphemy; see Lev. 24: 16, 'he that blasphemeth the name of the Lord, he shall surely be put to death'. In the Hebrew this is literally 'he who mentions the name of the Lord', and the LXX translates it 'he who names the name of the Lord'. It therefore seems unlikely that this sentence of the author's can be an Old Testament quotation. Perhaps the best suggestion is that the author is quoting an early Christian hymn. This is quite in line with his procedure elsewhere. The comparison of the false teachers with the Old Testament rebels would make us suspect that

Hymenaeus and Philetus were presbyters, as the rebels against Moses were Levites (the priestly caste).

20. This metaphor is certainly based on Rom. 9: 21–5. In that passage Paul is wrestling with the difficult problem of predestination, and is trying to answer the objection: 'If God always intended that the great majority of the Jews should fail to recognize the Messiah, how can you blame them for their failure?' He answers by suggesting that there are two sorts of people, 'vessels of mercy' and 'vessels of wrath'. The first sort were created by God to show the full extent of his mercy; the second sort were—Paul stops just short of saying 'created by God to show his retribution'. He does not say why they were created, but is content to point out that they do in fact show the operation of God's retribution. The author maintains that there are in the Church some who are destined to final loss, as well as those who are destined to eternal life, and he uses Paul's two classes of 'vessels' without observing the last-minute reservation of Paul, who will not say that God made the 'vessels of retribution'. For Paul the great problem was that God had apparently predestined some people to believe, and others to reject, God's promises; and God's will could not be rejected. But the author shows in the next verse that he is not aware of this problem at all, for he goes on to suggest quite innocently that one can *cleanse himself* and so become a 'vessel of mercy'. We may summarize the author's argument thus: 'There are these false teachers in the Church, doomed to destruction like the rebels of old. But do not be alarmed: in the household of God there must be some failures. You can by a little moral effort avoid these dangerous associations and become a useful vessel after all.'

21. *a man must cleanse himself from all those evil things.* The interpretation of verse 20 given above carries with it the conclusion that the reading in the N.E.B. footnote is to be preferred: 'a man must separate himself from these persons'.

22. *the wayward impulses of youth.* This could hardly apply

to the historical Timothy, who would be well beyond the range of such impulses by the end of Paul's career.

all who invoke the Lord. This simply means 'all Christians' and *the Lord* is Christ.

23. *foolish and ignorant speculations.* It would not be difficult to find modern forms of teaching that nicely fit this description. There are people calling themselves Christians who teach as gospel the most ignorant, fantastic, and useless speculations.

24. *the servant of the Lord.* Curiously enough, this exact phrase does not occur anywhere else in the New Testament, though there are plenty of examples of 'servant of Jesus Christ', and in 1 Pet. 2: 16 all Christians are called 'slaves (same word as *servant* here) in God's service'. The words here may be intended to designate the ordained ministers specially. See note on Titus 1: 1.

25. *and show them the truth,* literally 'to full knowledge of the truth', the same phrase as signifies baptism (we have claimed) in 1 Tim. 2: 4. But it can hardly mean that here, for the false teachers are surely baptized church members. This is what makes their rebellion so wrong.

26. *escape from the devil's snare, in which they have been caught and held at his will.* There are four possible ways of interpreting this sentence:

(*a*) 'escape from the devil's snare in which they have been caught by him, so as to do God's will';

(*b*) 'escape from the devil's snare, in which they have been caught by him so as to do his will';

(*c*) 'escape from the devil's snare, being recaptured by the servant of the Lord, so as to do God's will';

(*d*) 'escape from the devil's snare, caught now by God so as to do God's will'. Of these (*a*) is perhaps the best. ✻

WARNINGS AND ADVICE CONTINUED: 3: 1 — 4: 8

✻ It would be merely artificial to seek for any particular arrangement in this miscellaneous section. For the sake of convenience we follow the paragraphs as they occur in the N.E.B. ✻

DESCRIPTION OF THE FALSE TEACHERS

You must face the fact: the final age of this world is to be **3**
a time of troubles. Men will love nothing but money and **2**
self; they will be arrogant, boastful, and abusive; with
no respect for parents, no gratitude, no piety, no natural **3**
affection; they will be implacable in their hatreds,
scandal-mongers, intemperate and fierce, strangers to all
goodness, traitors, adventurers, swollen with self-impor- **4**
tance. They will be men who put pleasure in the place of
God, men who preserve the outward form of religion, **5**
but are a standing denial of its reality. Keep clear of men
like these. They are the sort that insinuate themselves into **6**
private houses and there get miserable women into their
clutches, women burdened with a sinful past, and led on
by all kinds of desires, who are always wanting to be **7**
taught, but are incapable of reaching a knowledge of the
truth. As Jannes and Jambres defied Moses, so these men **8**
defy the truth; they have lost the power to reason, and
they cannot pass the tests of faith. But their successes will **9**
be short-lived, for, like those opponents of Moses, they
will come to be recognized by everyone for the fools they
are.

✻ 1. *the final age of this world is to be a time of troubles.* This belief
runs all through early Christian literature, and is an inheritance
from Jewish thought. See Matt. 24: 21, 'It will be a time of
great distress, such as has never been from the beginning of
the world until now'. But the author of the Pastorals does not
lay great stress on the fact that the appearance of false teachers
heralds the end of the world. In the Pastorals there is no very
strong expectation that the world will end soon, and this
suggests that they were written at a period when the Church

was to some extent settling down to an indefinitely-continuing life in the world, and losing its first strong conviction that the world was to end soon.

2–5.   There follows a list of unpleasant qualities, mostly consisting of single words in the Greek. The list seems to be based on the list of vices found in the pagan world which Paul gives in Rom. 1: 29–31. There are very few adjectives or phrases in the author's list that do not find a parallel, more or less exact, in Paul's. A remarkable parallel can also be found in Philo for the first phrase in the list and the last phrase in verse 4. Philo was a philosophically-minded Jew of Alexandria who died about A.D. 50. His works were probably not known to Paul, but they were certainly known to the author of the Letter to Hebrews, and probably also to the author of the Fourth Gospel. Philo writes in one passage of men who are 'lovers of self rather than lovers of God', and in another of men who are 'lovers of pleasure and sensual things rather than lovers of virtue and of God'. The resemblance is blurred in the N.E.B. translation, but in fact the author shares with Philo no less than three very unusual adjectives. Thus the list of unpleasant characters to be expected in *the final age* proves to be a more conventional one than might appear at first sight. It has often been pointed out that, whereas Paul's list is a vivid and forceful description of the non-Christian world of his day, the author's list apparently refers exclusively to bad characters within the Church (see verse 5).

6–7.   These verses seem to describe a fashionable religious teacher. Just such a type is described by Irenaeus (about A.D. 180–200). Marcus, a Gnostic teacher, courted rich women by telling them they had the gift of prophecy, seduced them, and made off with their money.

insinuate themselves into private houses. Compare Jude 4, 'certain persons who have wormed their way in'. There is quite a striking resemblance between Jude and the Pastorals; see, for example, Jude 3, 'the faith which God entrusted to his people once and for all', and compare 1 Tim. 6: 20; Jude 11, the reference to Korah's rebellion, with which compare 2 Tim. 2: 19; Jude 18, 'In the final age there will be men who pour scorn on religion', and see 1 Tim. 4: 1; and Jude 24–5, which is very probably a liturgical extract and reminds us of the many such extracts in the Pastorals.

8. *As Jannes and Jambres defied Moses.* These are two Egyptian magicians, not mentioned in the Old Testament, figures belonging to Jewish legend. There is a reference to them, probably earlier than this, in one of the Qumran documents, written by the community of whose activities we learn from the Dead Sea Scrolls. But later rabbinic writings give us fuller information about them. They are represented as having suggested to Pharaoh the plan to kill the Hebrew babies (see Exod. 1: 15–22), and they are numbered among the magicians mentioned in Exod. 7: 11 and 22 as to some extent rivalling Moses in the production of wonders. *Jambres* was probably originally Mambres, and this in its turn was not really a name at first, but a description meaning 'the apostate'. But 'Jannes the apostate' by a misunderstanding turned into two individuals, Jannes and Jambres, when translated into Greek.

9. *like those opponents of Moses, they will come to be recognized by everyone for the fools they are.* This must refer to some definite incident in the legendary career of Jannes and Jambres. The most likely is that mentioned in Exod. 8: 16–19, where the magicians are unable to turn the dust to lice, as Moses did, and confess that 'This is the finger of God'. The author of the Book of Wisdom, in commenting on this event, though he does not mention the two magicians, uses the word rendered *fools* here in connexion with the Egyptians' idol worship (see Wisdom 15: 18 — 16: 1). Origen (died A.D. 255) tells us that in his day there was a Greek book which gave a life of Jannes and Jambres. The author of the Pastorals must have known this book, or an earlier version of it. ✻

WHAT THE CHRISTIAN LEADER MUST EXPECT

10 But you, my son, have followed, step by step, my teaching and my manner of life, my resolution, my faith,
11 patience, and spirit of love, and my fortitude under persecutions and sufferings—all that I went through at Antioch, at Iconium, at Lystra, all the persecutions I
12 endured; and the Lord rescued me out of them all. Yes, persecution will come to all who want to live a godly life
13 as Christians, whereas wicked men and charlatans will make progress from bad to worse, deceiving and deceived.
14 But for your part, stand by the truths you have learned and are assured of. Remember from whom you learned
15 them; remember that from early childhood you have been familiar with the sacred writings which have power to make you wise and lead you to salvation through faith in
16 Christ Jesus. Every inspired scripture has its use for teaching the truth and refuting error, or for reformation of
17 manners and discipline in right living, so that the man who belongs to God may be efficient and equipped for good work of every kind.

✵ 10–13. It is very difficult to believe that this passage comes from Paul's pen. In the first place, Paul seems to be praising himself in a way very unlike such passages as 2 Corinthians, chapters 10 and 11, where he mentions his sufferings and achievements only in order to declare passionately that such boasting is the mark of a fool. Then there is the mixture here of different kinds of objects that Timothy has followed, and the vague reference to past events. All these indications suggest a later writer. The events referred to are related in Acts, chapters 13 and 14, adventures of Paul which all took place before he enlisted Timothy in his team of missionaries (see

Acts 16: 1–3). If this were really Paul writing, it would seem more natural to refer to adventures which Paul and Timothy had shared.

12. *to live a godly life*. Here is the adjective connected with that word *eusebeia* which we have noted as being such a favourite of the author's. It is a most unPauline phrase.

13. *charlatans*, literally 'wizards'; some have suggested that the Gnostic teachers actually practised magic. Both the reference just above to the wizards Jannes and Jambres, and the probable meaning of 'busybodies' in 1 Tim. 5: 13 would confirm this. But the meaning given in the N.E.B. is often met with in contemporary literature, and is probably right here.

15. *from early childhood you have been familiar with the sacred writings*. This refers of course to the Old Testament. We must remember that Timothy was the child of a 'mixed marriage', a marriage between people of different religions, and such homes are not usually remarkable for piety.

16. *Every inspired scripture has its use for teaching the truth*. That word *inspired* is unique in the Bible; it seems to be drawn from the vocabulary of Greek religion, according to which sacred writers were the mere tools of God, with no initiative of their own. The word translated *scripture* can only mean 'passage of scripture', not 'book of the Bible'. We might therefore translate the phrase better thus: 'Every passage in scripture is inspired, and is therefore useful for teaching.' This sentence seems to be modelled on Rom. 15: 4. We can compare them side by side:

Rom. 15: 4	2 Tim. 3: 16
For all the ancient scriptures were written for our own *instruction*, in order that through the *encouragement* they give us we may maintain our hope with *fortitude*.	*Every inspired scripture has* its use for *teaching* the truth and refuting error, or for *reformation* of manners and *discipline* in right living.

Corresponding words in the two passages are printed in italics. There is also a remarkable parallel to this passage in 2 Timothy to be found in the works of Epictetus, a Stoic philosopher who wrote in A.D. 90. He says that the mysteries of the pagan religions exist for the purpose of 'discipline and reformation of manners'. It almost seems as if the author were adapting Paul's sentence in Rom. 15: 4 to his own situation, and inserting into it a touch of contemporary pagan morality.

17. *the man who belongs to God.* Probably not to be distinguished from the 'man of God' of 1 Tim. 6: 11. Both phrases indicate the church leader. ✶

FINAL CHARGE TO TIMOTHY

4 Before God, and before Christ Jesus who is to judge men living and dead, I adjure you by his coming appearance 2 and his reign, proclaim the message, press it home on all occasions, convenient or inconvenient, use argument, reproof, and appeal, with all the patience that the work of 3 teaching requires. For the time will come when they will not stand wholesome teaching, but will follow their own fancy and gather a crowd of teachers to tickle their ears. 4 They will stop their ears to the truth and turn to mytho- 5 logy. But you yourself must keep calm and sane at all times; face hardship, work to spread the Gospel, and do all the duties of your calling.

✶ We do not take this as an authentic charge from Paul. It is rather what the author thought Paul might have said.

1. *Before God, and before Christ Jesus who is to judge men living and dead.* Probably a phrase from a creed; compare Acts 10: 42, 'he is the one who has been designated by God as judge of the living and the dead'; and 1 Pet. 4: 5, 'him who stands ready to pass judgement on the living and the dead'. Indeed

some scholars think that the whole of this passage was originally part of a baptismal address.

2.   *press it home on all occasions, convenient and inconvenient.* This could mean 'when you feel inclined and when you do not', in which case the N.E.B. footnote reading is better: 'be on duty at all times'. But it could mean 'whether men are anxious to hear or not', which goes better with the translation in the text. On the whole the latter makes better sense.

3.   The author must be thinking of the Gnostic teachers, who offered special instruction for the *élite*, calculated to appeal to certain types of mind. One could well apply this verse to our own day: very often a new exponent of Christianity is listened to more because he is 'radical' or 'challenging' than because what he says has any very close relationship to what we find in the New Testament.

5.   *keep calm and sane.* Only one word in Greek: 'be sober'.

work to spread the Gospel, literally 'do the work of an evangelist'; compare Eph. 4: 11, 'some to be apostles, some prophets, some evangelists'.

do all the duties of your calling, literally 'fulfil your *diakonia*'. This is a great word in the New Testament, meaning Christian service in the widest sense, stemming from the supreme service for mankind which Jesus Christ came to do (see Mark 10: 45). ✳

AN EXTRACT FROM A GENUINE LETTER OF PAUL,
PLACED IN A LATER CONTEXT

As for me, already my life is being poured out on the altar, 6
and the hour for my departure is upon me. I have run the 7
great race, I have finished the course, I have kept faith.
And now the prize awaits me, the garland of righteousness 8
which the Lord, the all-just Judge, will award me on that
great Day; and it is not for me alone, but for all who
have set their hearts on his coming appearance.

Do your best to join me soon; for Demas has deserted 9, 10

me because his heart was set on this world; he has gone to
11 Thessalonica, Crescens to Galatia, Titus to Dalmatia; I have
no one with me but Luke. Pick up Mark and bring him with
12 you, for I find him a useful assistant. Tychicus I have sent
13 to Ephesus. When you come, bring the cloak I left with
Carpus at Troas, and the books, above all my notebooks.
14   Alexander the copper-smith did me a great deal of
harm. Retribution will fall upon him from the Lord.
15 You had better be on your guard against him too, for he
16 violently opposed everything I said. At the first hearing
of my case no one came into court to support me; they
all left me in the lurch; I pray that it may not be held
17 against them. But the Lord stood by me and lent me
strength, so that I might be his instrument in making the
full proclamation of the Gospel for the whole pagan world
to hear; and thus I was rescued out of the lion's jaws.
18 And the Lord will rescue me from every attempt to do
me harm, and keep me safe until his heavenly reign begins. Glory to him for ever and ever! Amen.
19   Greetings to Prisca and Aquila, and the household of
Onesiphorus.
20   Erastus stayed behind at Corinth, and I left Trophimus
21 ill at Miletus. Do try to get here before winter.
Greetings from Eubulus, Pudens, Linus, and Claudia,
and from all the brotherhood here.
22   The Lord be with your spirit. Grace be with you all!

* Very many scholars take verses 6–8 as part of Paul's genuine
letter also, but these verses are not so taken here. We prefer
to take them as a fine tribute on the part of the author to Paul,
apostle and martyr. This is partly because the verses which
follow these do not seem to have been written just before

Paul's execution, as these verses claim to have been written; but as well as this there are sentiments and phrases in the passage that do not look like Paul's. In his genuine letters Paul does not show such confidence in his reward; and that word *epiphany* in verse 8 is not used in a Pauline sense.

6. *my life is being poured out on the altar.* Paul uses this metaphor of himself in Phil. 2: 17, which may be literally translated 'even if I am being poured out on the offering and service of your faith'. But this is the very letter in which Paul shows the greatest diffidence about his own salvation (see Phil. 3: 12–16).

the hour for my departure is upon me. The word for *departure* means literally 'unloosing', as of a ship slipping her cable. The custom was to pour out a libation or drink-offering to the gods just before weighing anchor. Paul uses a verb from the same root in Phil. 1: 23, 'what I should like is to depart and be with Christ'. The use of the noun to mean 'death', as here, is not found before Clement's letter.

7. *I have run the great race, I have finished the course.* Paul uses similar, though not identical, language in Phil. 2: 16 and 3: 14, 'I did not run my race in vain' and 'I press towards the goal to win the prize'. The conclusion we draw is that the author has borrowed the thought, and to some extent the language, from Paul in Philippians.

8. *the garland of righteousness which the Lord, the all-just Judge, will award me.* In the Greek the words *righteousness* and *all-just* (an English word which the N.E.B. seems to have invented) are from the same root. This is not Pauline theology. Paul taught that God's righteousness is ours in Christ now.

who have set their hearts on his coming appearance, literally 'who have loved his appearance', a very unPauline phrase.

9–22. Genuine words of Paul. We are assuming that this letter was written from Rome to Timothy in Asia Minor soon after the beginning of Paul's second and last imprisonment in Rome. This carries with it the implication that the 'captivity' letters, Colossians and Philemon, were written from Rome well before this, towards the end of Paul's first imprisonment.

(Philippians we assume to be earlier, and Ephesians not to be by Paul at all.) This fragment of a letter must come fairly soon after a period of freedom, for it is full of references to recent free activity. It cannot have been written with the immediate prospect of death before him, for Paul expects to be able to welcome Timothy after the long journey from Asia Minor to Rome, and several other friends likewise. This situation, however, is not at all improbable, and is on the whole a more likely reconstruction of the events than the alternative, which is to maintain that the author invented all these elaborate (and, as far as he was concerned, pointless) details about Paul.

9. *Do your best to join me soon.* But even if Paul's letter were to be delivered as soon as possible and Timothy were to set off at once, and travel with all possible speed, there would have to be an interval of several months before Paul could hope to see Timothy. So Paul was not expecting immediate death.

10. *Demas has deserted me.* No doubt the same man mentioned, together with Luke, in Col. 4: 14. At the time of the writing of Colossians he was with Paul in Rome; we assume that his desertion has taken place since. A copyist in a manuscript preserved in the Medici Library at Florence adds in the margin the information that Demas became the priest of a pagan temple at Thessalonica. On what authority he says this we do not know.

Crescens is only mentioned here.

Galatia normally means a region in Asia Minor colonized by Gauls some centuries earlier, but it could mean Gaul, roughly modern France, and to this meaning the reading *Gallia* in the N.E.B. footnote testifies. But on the whole Galatia in Asia Minor is more likely.

Titus. A companion of Paul since early days (see Gal. 2: 1–3). He is also frequently mentioned in 2 Corinthians, since he played an important part in the sometimes painful exchanges that took place between Paul and the Church in Corinth. In Rom. 15: 19 we learn that the gospel had reached Illyricum, which lay in the direction of *Dalmatia*, and may even have been reckoned part of it. In Titus 3: 12 Paul appears to be writing from Nicopolis in Dalmatia, or at least to be intending to meet fellow-workers there. This is a passage in the letter to Titus which we regard as genuinely written by Paul.

11. *Luke* is mentioned wherever Demas is in Colossians and Philemon. There is no reason to doubt that this is the Luke who later wrote both Gospel and Acts. We learn from Col. 4: 14 that he was a doctor.

Mark. This must be the Mark who went with Paul and Barnabas on their first missionary journey. See Acts 12: 25, where they take John Mark with them. In Acts 13: 13 we learn that John Mark returned to Jerusalem in the middle of the tour, and in Acts 15: 36–9 we have the incident of the disagreement between Paul and Barnabas that arose just because of this desertion. Both from this reference in the Pastorals, and from Col. 4: 10, we must conclude that Paul was now reconciled to Mark, and probably had been for some time before this was written. These three persons, Demas, Luke, and Mark, all seem to have some connexion with Colossae, for all send greetings to the Colossians. Perhaps Timothy was at Colossae when this letter, of which we have a fragment here, was written. But see below on Tychicus.

12. *Tychicus*, as we have seen, is mentioned in the letter to the Colossians, where he is no doubt the bearer of the letter to the Church at Colossae from Rome. He is also mentioned in Eph. 6: 21, and in Acts 20: 4, where he is described as an Asian, and is probably a member of a party of church delegates bringing to Jerusalem their contributions to the fund organized by Paul in aid of needy Christians in Judaea.

I have sent to Ephesus. This seems to imply that Timothy was not at Ephesus when this letter was written; otherwise Paul would surely have said 'I have sent to you at Ephesus', or more likely would have assumed that Tychicus would arrive before his letter could. Ephesus and Colossae were about 130 miles apart as the crow flies, but there was frequent intercourse between them.

13. *the cloak.* A large enveloping garment with a hole at the top for the head to pass through. One editor thoughtfully supplies two modern analogies, calculated to appeal to both religious and non-religious; he says it is 'like a chasuble or bicycle cape'. It could mean a cover for books or parchments, and some have accepted this sense here; but the former seems more likely.

Troas. A sea port on the north-west corner of Asia Minor. Paul must have passed through it often in his days of freedom (see, for example, Acts 20: 4–12). Its mention here shows that Timothy was expected to travel overland across Greece, and only to make the sea passage from Dalmatia to Italy.

the books, above all my notebooks. Two quite different words in Greek; the first is *biblia* (from which our word 'Bible' comes). The second means literally 'the parchments'. The first word might refer to papyrus rolls, on which less important documents were written. The parchments might be expected to contain more important material. Probably the parchments contained Paul's version of the Old Testament in Greek, no small burden to carry around. But some scholars (including presumably the translators of the N.E.B.) think that they were unused rolls of parchment suitable for Paul's correspondence. Others have suggested that the *biblia* were in fact Paul's personal documents, including perhaps his certificate of Roman citizenship. In any case it is unlikely that so ambiguous a phrase would have been invented by a later author.

14. *Alexander the copper-smith.* It is unlikely that he is identical with either the false teacher of 1 Tim. 1: 20, or the Jewish spokesman of Acts 19:33. The phrase translated *did me a great deal of harm* is literally 'informed many evil things against me', and the regular word for an informer is connected with this verb. One scholar makes the attractive suggestion that this incident happened in Troas, so Timothy is warned to avoid Alexander when he does pass through Troas. It may even be that Troas was where Paul was arrested.

16. *At the first hearing.* This was known as the *prima actio*, a preliminary process at which it was to be decided whether

the case was to be proceeded with or not. There must have been a verdict of *non liquet*, 'the matter is not clear', for Paul was neither condemned out of hand nor released.

17. *out of the lion's jaws.* Perhaps there had been a possibility of Paul's being condemned and punished on the spot. By *the lion* Paul may mean just danger generally, or the devil, as in 1 Pet. 5: 8, or even the Roman power. The Jewish historian Josephus tells us that when the Emperor Tiberius died in the year A.D. 37, the news reached Herod Agrippa in the cryptic form 'the lion is dead'.

18. We treat this verse as a pious addition by the author, on the grounds that 'into his heavenly kingdom' (N.E.B., footnote, which is on the whole better than the N.E.B. text) is not really in accordance with Paul's usage. Also it seems to contain echoes of the Lord's Prayer, which suggests a liturgical origin.

19. *Prisca and Aquila.* First heard of in Acts 18: 2 (where Prisca is called Priscilla), when they arrive in Ephesus having been recently expelled from Rome. Paul was perhaps the means of converting them to Christianity from Judaism. In Rom. 16: 3 Paul sends them a greeting from Corinth, apparently to Rome. But many scholars hold that the sixteenth chapter of Romans is not an integral part of that Letter, but was tacked on later. For this some textual evidence can be found. It is certainly part of a letter of Paul's; some have suggested that it was originally sent to Ephesus. The many greetings to friends would suit this. If so, then we may assume that Prisca and Aquila are still in Ephesus, and that Paul knows a letter to Colossae will be read in Ephesus also.

the household of Onesiphorus. See note on 1: 16. Our reconstruction of Paul's movements as reflected in this fragment of a letter requires that Onesiphorus should have visited Rome since Paul's arrival there for the second time as a prisoner, spent some time in searching for him, found him and visited him frequently, and then died. If so, Paul is not writing *immediately* after the beginning of his second imprisonment.

But an interval of a few weeks, perhaps two months at the least, would allow for Onesiphorus' history as reflected in the Pastorals, and such an interval is not incompatible with our other suggestions.

20. *Erastus.* In Acts 19: 22 he is mentioned as one of Paul's assistants who is sent on a mission to Macedonia. In Rom. 16: 23 he sends greetings from Corinth. If our suggestion is right, that Romans, chapter 16, is really directed to Ephesus, all this would fit in well enough.

I left Trophimus ill at Miletus. Trophimus is mentioned in Acts 20: 4, where he is a member of the same party as Tychicus. They call at Miletus, but we learn that on that occasion Trophimus at least arrived in Jerusalem, for in Acts 21: 29 we read that the Jews had seen him in company with Paul at Jerusalem. His illness at Miletus therefore cannot have occurred during that particular journey. But we have allowed plenty of time in which this might have happened during the period of Paul's first release.

21. *Eubulus, Pudens, Linus, and Claudia.* Not mentioned elsewhere in the New Testament, but *Linus* occurs in succession lists of bishops of Rome as coming next after Peter and Paul, who are regarded as having founded the Church of Rome. These lists cannot be regarded as conclusive evidence that there were bishops (in the later sense) in Rome as early as the first century A.D. On the whole it seems more likely that the office of bishop as we know it was not clearly existing in Rome before the end of the first quarter of the second century. But Linus might well have occupied the same position as Clement held a generation later, the spokesman and secretary of the presbyters in Rome. As such he would naturally be taken for the bishop by Christians composing a succession list more than a hundred years after his time. As far as it goes, this is a small piece of evidence that this part of the letter was written from Rome. ✳

✳ ✳ ✳ ✳ ✳ ✳ ✳ ✳ ✳ ✳ ✳ ✳ ✳

THE LETTER TO TITUS

✻   ✻   ✻   ✻   ✻   ✻   ✻   ✻   ✻   ✻   ✻   ✻   ✻

Training for the Christian Life

ADDRESS

1 FROM PAUL, servant of God and apostle of Jesus Christ, marked as such by faith and knowledge and hope—the faith of God's chosen people, knowledge of the truth as
2 our religion has it, and the hope of eternal life. Yes, it is eternal life that God, who cannot lie, promised long ages
3 ago, and now in his own good time he has openly declared himself in the proclamation which was entrusted to me by ordinance of God our Saviour.

4 To Titus, my true-born son in the faith which we share, grace and peace from God our Father and Christ Jesus our Saviour.

* This is the longest of the three addresses, but it is also the most obscure. It seems to be based on phrases from the other two letters.

1. *servant of God.* Strangely enough, this phrase does not occur anywhere else in the New Testament. Paul often calls himself a servant of Christ.

faith and knowledge and hope. The N.E.B. has made a determined effort to give a clear, theological interpretation to a phrase which is vague and loose-knit in the Greek. It runs literally: 'according to the faith of the elect of God and to the full knowledge of the truth according to piety in hope of eternal life'. Probably the following explanation (offered by one scholar) is the best: '"according to" defines the sphere in which Paul exercises his apostleship; the aim of his work is to increase the faith, the knowledge, and the hope of his converts'. But one must bear in mind the possibility that the author had no such clear scheme in mind, and is merely linking familiar phrases with the general intention of expanding the meaning of 'apostleship'.

knowledge of the truth. This is the same phrase as we encountered in I Tim. 2: 4 and Heb. 10: 26, in both of which places we have suggested that it implies instruction leading to baptism. This may well be the implication here also.

2. *God, who cannot lie*. Compare Heb. 6: 18, 'Here, then, are two irrevocable acts in which God could not possibly play us false'.

3. This verse seems to be a mixture of Rom. 16: 26 'by eternal God's command' and I Tim. I: I 'by command of God our Saviour'. It may also be inspired by the hymn in 2 Tim. I: 9–10.

4. *the faith which we share* probably means the faith common to Jews and Gentiles. Compare Jude 3, 'our salvation— which is yours no less than ours'.

Christ Jesus our Saviour. Most remarkably, the author applies the title *Saviour* to both God the Father and Jesus Christ in two consecutive verses. Both usages are of course perfectly consistent with Christian doctrine, but to bring them together like this, without any particular significance, is surely the mark of a not very clear mind, and an indication that we do not have Paul's work here. ✲

RIGHT CONDUCT FOR VARIOUS CLASSES IN
THE CHURCH: I: 5 — 2: IO

✲ After the Address, the letter falls roughly into three parts: a section dealing with right conduct (this one); then a section dealing with doctrine, in so far as we can describe the author as teaching doctrine at all (2: 11 — 3: 11); and finally a brief extract from a genuine letter of Paul's (3: 12–15). But the first two parts are fairly miscellaneous, and we find some doctrine in the first and some teaching about conduct in the second. ✲

THE ORDAINED MINISTERS AND FALSE TEACHERS

5 My intention in leaving you behind in Crete was that you should set in order what was left over, and in particular should institute elders in each town. In doing so,
6 observe the tests I prescribed: is he a man of unimpeachable character, faithful to his one wife, the father of children who are believers, who are under no imputa-
7 tion of loose living, and are not out of control? For as God's steward a bishop must be a man of unimpeachable character. He must not be overbearing or short-tempered; he must be no drinker, no brawler, no money-grubber,
8 but hospitable, right-minded, temperate, just, devout,
9 and self-controlled. He must adhere to the true doctrine, so that he may be well able both to move his hearers with wholesome teaching and to confute objectors.

10 There are all too many, especially among Jewish converts, who are out of all control; they talk wildly and
11 lead men's minds astray. Such men must be curbed, because they are ruining whole families by teaching
12 things they should not, and all for sordid gain. It was a Cretan prophet, one of their own countrymen, who said, 'Cretans were always liars, vicious brutes, lazy gluttons'—
13 and he told the truth! All the more reason why you should pull them up sharply, so that they may come to a
14 sane belief, instead of lending their ears to Jewish myths and commandments of merely human origin, the work of men who turn their backs upon the truth.

15 To the pure all things are pure; but nothing is pure to the tainted minds of disbelievers, tainted alike in reason
16 and conscience. They profess to acknowledge God, but

deny him by their actions. Their detestable obstinacy disqualifies them for any good work.

✲ 5–9.   Advice on the choice of Presbyter-Bishops.

5.   *leaving you behind in Crete*. The only hint in the New Testament of any other connexion between Paul and Crete is Acts 27: 7–9, where the ship in which Paul is travelling shelters in the lee of Crete for a short time. But that can have no connexion with the visit implied here. As we have seen, there was plenty of time for Paul to have visited the island in between the two Roman captivities.

set in order what was left over. A vague phrase, found also in Philo.

institute elders in each town. The word *elders* is literally 'presbyters'. In the advice which follows, the author begins by writing of *elders* in the plural, then goes on with the words *is he a man of unimpeachable character* etc., and in verse 7 we read *a bishop must be a man of unimpeachable character* etc. This has occasioned much dispute: some argue that the identity of presbyter and bishop is clear here; others that we must understand the words thus: 'Presbyters must be well behaved [because from them the bishop must be chosen]; the bishop must be a man of good character, etc.' The solution adopted in this commentary is to assume that the author knew of the identity of bishops and presbyters in Paul's day, but wished his words also to apply to the situation in his own day, when the bishop as such had emerged, or was emerging.

6.   *is he a man of unimpeachable character* . . .. This list of desirable qualities is very like that given in 1 Tim. 3: 1–7. We concluded there that the author drew all his lists from some one original list, not necessarily of Christian origin at all.

faithful to his one wife. See note on 1 Tim. 3: 2.

the father of children who are believers. It is assumed that the clergy will be married. The notion that clergy should be celibate had not yet occurred to anyone.

7. *as God's steward*. Compare 1 Cor. 4: 1, 'stewards of the secrets of God'.

no money-grubber. This probably means that he should not take up a trade unsuitable to his position as bishop, rather than that he should not make money out of his office.

9. After this verse one manuscript adds the following: 'He must not appoint men who have been through the divorce courts nor make them deacons; nor should [his nominees] have wives who have previously been divorced. Nor must such people be permitted to serve the Almighty in the sanctuary. As God's servant, reprove rulers who are unrighteous judges, who take bribes, who tell lies, and who shew no mercy.' This must have been originally an addition by some copyist who wished to introduce material suitable to his church situation. It is remarkable that there is no mention of deacons in Titus.

10. There is evidence that there was a strong community of Jews at this time in Crete. But, as this part of the letter does not seem to have been written by Paul, we must imagine that these remarks are aimed chiefly at Jewish teaching in the author's own area, probably Asia Minor.

11. *they are ruining whole families*. Probably to be taken in the same sense as 2 Tim. 3: 6.

teaching things they should not. The phrase in Greek resembles that used in 1 Tim. 5: 13, 'speaking of things better left unspoken'. There we suggested that it referred to magical practices, and the same implication may very well be present here also.

12. *a Cretan prophet*. The prophet in question is Epimenides, who seems to have lived about 500 B.C. He gained a reputation for prophecy because he foretold the failure of the Persian expedition against Greece ten years before it took place. It happened in 490 B.C. The quotation given here is probably not taken direct from Epimenides, but from Callimachus, a poet who wrote a long poem called 'Minos' in the third century B.C. His may also be the poem quoted by Paul in

Acts 17: 28, 'for in him we live and move, in him we exist'. Callimachus incidentally tells us in his poem how the Cretans gained their reputation for lying. They claimed to have in their island the tomb of Zeus, king of the gods. Callimachus indignantly refutes this claim, and addresses Zeus thus: 'Cretans were always liars, for they have invented thy tomb, Lord. Thou didst not die, but livest for ever.' Cretans were thus labelled as liars, and 'to play the Cretan' meant to lie. The author uses this popular belief in order to impale the false teachers on the horns of a dilemma: either they accept the truth of the quotation and stand self-condemned; or else they deny it and condemn their own prophet. It is very difficult to believe that Paul would use so childish a device for refuting opponents. The author, however, may have an ulterior object in mind: perhaps the false teaching with which he is in contact originated in Crete, and he uses the quotation from Epimenides to discredit all things Cretan.

14. *Jewish myths*. The teaching seems very like that condemned in Paul's letter to the Colossians, a mixture of Judaism and Gnosticism. The *myths* may have consisted of Gnostic elaborations of Old Testament stories.

15. *To the pure all things are pure*. The simple phrase 'all things are pure' occurs in Rom. 14: 20 (where the N.E.B. translates it 'Everything is pure in itself'). There it seems to be a slogan of the 'enlightened' party, whom Paul warns not to shock the consciences of the 'unenlightened' needlessly. But the author here uses it against the Jewish teachers, who were labelling certain things as impure in themselves. This was of course only in accord with the Law of Moses, which does precisely this; see Leviticus, chapter 11.

tainted minds. The author has a habit of assuming that those who disagree with him must be morally wrong as well as intellectually mistaken.

16. *They profess to acknowledge God*. Compare 2 Tim. 3: 5.

Their detestable obstinacy. The Greek is literally 'being detestable and disobedient and unfit for any good work'. It looks very much as if the author is simply piling on abusive epithets indiscriminately. ✻

RIGHT CONDUCT FOR MEN, WOMEN, AND SLAVES

2 For your own part, what you say must be in keeping with
2 wholesome doctrine. Let the older men know that they should be sober, high-principled, and temperate, sound
3 in faith, in love, and in endurance. The older women, similarly, should be reverent in their bearing, not scandal-mongers or slaves to strong drink; they must set a high
4 standard, and school the younger women to be loving
5 wives and mothers, temperate, chaste, and kind, busy at home, respecting the authority of their own husbands. Thus the Gospel will not be brought into disrepute.
6,7 Urge the younger men, similarly, to be temperate in all things, and set them a good example yourself. In your teaching, you must show integrity and high principle,
8 and use wholesome speech to which none can take excep-tion. This will shame any opponent, when he finds not a word to say to our discredit.
9 Tell slaves to respect their masters' authority in every-thing, and to comply with their demands without answer-
10 ing back; not to pilfer, but to show themselves strictly honest and trustworthy; for in all such ways they will add lustre to the doctrine of God our Saviour.

✻ 1. *wholesome doctrine.* It is remarkable that the advice which follows has very little to do with Christian doctrine as such, but consists of precepts appropriate to almost any set of people who wished to be respectable in the eyes of the author's contemporaries. The author was certainly not much interested in theology as such.

3. *The older women.* This list of qualities is very like that given in 1 Tim. 3: 11 for the wives of deacons.

reverent in their bearing. The word translated *reverent* is literally 'priestlike', so that perhaps 'reverend' would be nearer the sense. Knox translates 'carry themselves as befits a holy calling'; but it is more likely that the word echoes 1 Tim. 2: 9, 'Women again must dress in becoming manner', and refers to their dress as much as to their conduct. There may be the thought of a sort of natural priesthood of older women.

they must set a high standard. Rather a loose translation for a word which means literally 'one who is a good teacher'.

4. *and school the younger women to be loving wives.* A common conventional description of women on contemporary funeral monuments is 'a loving wife and a woman of discipline' (same root as *school* here), so the author seems to have achieved literally something like Mrs Malaprop's 'nice derangement of epitaphs'! Philo has a very similar phrase for the ideal wife.

5. *busy at home.* A rare word, not found again till some time after this. A well-supported alternative reading is a very similar word meaning 'housekeepers'. Several scholars prefer this reading, and take it with what is the next word in the Greek, to give the sense 'good housekeepers'. There is much to be said for this, as the author does not elsewhere use 'good' by itself in a list of desirable qualities.

respecting the authority of their own husbands. Compare Eph. 5: 22, 'Wives, be subject to your husbands'; and 1 Tim. 2: 11, 'A woman must be a learner, listening quietly and with due submission'. To Westerners this view of woman's status will seem very old fashioned; to Eastern Christians it will seem perfectly obvious. Both need to rethink the question in the light of what Paul says about there being neither male nor female in Christ. But this passage will hardly provide any great insight.

7. *set them a good example yourself.* The advice given to Titus here is very like that given to Timothy in 1 Tim. 4: 12; it

suggests that both Timothy and Titus are ideal figures in the Pastorals, and that the advice is really intended for church leaders of a later age.

8. *This will shame any opponent*, literally 'the man in opposition', not the devil, as the parallel in 1 Pet. 3: 16 shows, 'Keep your conscience clear, so that when you are abused, those who malign your Christian conduct may be put to shame'.

9. *Tell slaves to respect their masters' authority*. Teaching for slaves has already been given in 1 Tim. 6: 1–2, and can also be found in Col. 3: 22–5, in Eph. 6: 5–8, and in 1 Pet. 2: 18–25. If we add to these passages 1 Pet. 5: 1–5, where advice is given to other classes of people as well, we can see a pattern of Christian instruction emerging. These 'domestic codes', as they are called, can be found also in contemporary pagan ethical instruction. The difference lies not so much in the virtues commended as in the motive behind the conduct. This comes out much more clearly in 1 Peter than in the Pastorals. See 1 Pet. 2: 20–1, 'But when you have behaved well and suffer for it, your fortitude is a fine thing in the sight of God. To that you were called, because Christ suffered on your behalf, and thereby left you an example; it is for you to follow in his steps.'

10. *they will add lustre to the doctrine of God our Saviour*. Christianity is here equated with the teaching. The thought is a fine one: even slaves can be powerful witnesses to Christ. But the language is most unlike that of Paul, who never speaks of Christianity as consisting of 'the teaching of God'. ✳

FUNDAMENTAL DOCTRINES OF CHRISTIANITY:
2: 11 — 3: 11

✳ This section has more doctrine in it than the last. It does mention the incarnation and redemption, both in 2: 13–14 and in 3: 3–8 and, it includes a remarkable reference to baptism. But by the end of the section the author has fallen back on his customary denunciation of false teaching, and in between the two doctrinal passages comes some simple ethical teaching (3: 1–2). ✽

THE PURPOSE OF THE INCARNATION

For the grace of God has dawned upon the world with 11 healing for all mankind; and by it we are disciplined to 12 renounce godless ways and worldly desires, and to live a life of temperance, honesty, and godliness in the present age, looking forward to the happy fulfilment of our hopes 13 when the splendour of our great God and Saviour Christ Jesus will appear. He it is who sacrificed himself for us, to 14 set us free from all wickedness and to make us a pure people marked out for his own, eager to do good.

✽ The language of these verses sounds liturgical; the Old Testament quotations in verse 14 point in the same direction. Have we here perhaps an extract from a prayer used at the eucharist or at baptism? Compare 1 Pet. 2: 9, which is built on much the same pattern: 'But you are a chosen race, a royal priesthood, a dedicated nation, and a people claimed by God for his own, to proclaim the triumphs of him who has called you out of darkness into his marvellous light.' Many scholars believe that 1 Peter contains a baptismal liturgy.

11. *with healing for all mankind.* Notice the emphasis on the universality of salvation, one of the author's finest insights.

12. *by it we are disciplined to renounce godless ways and worldly desires.* This is hardly Paul's gospel. The phrase *worldly desires* is quite uncharacteristic of Paul. The nearest parallels are 1 John 2: 15–17, 'Do not set your hearts on the godless world'; and 2 Pet. 1: 4, 'you may escape the corruption with which lust (same word as *desires*) has infected the world'. The exact phrase *worldly desires* is used in 2 Clement 17: 3, a work which may well be quoting this passage.

13. *when the splendour of our great God and Saviour Christ Jesus will appear*. The translation in the N.E.B. footnote is 'when the splendour of the great God and our Saviour Christ Jesus shall appear', so it is possible to translate this passage in such a way as to avoid applying the word God directly to Jesus. It is true that New Testament writers on the whole avoid such a usage. This is not because they thought that Jesus was less than God, but because to call him God frequently and indiscriminately would run the risk of identifying him completely with God the Father. 'The great God' was occasionally used in Jewish writings intended for Gentiles, when Gentiles were represented as referring to the God of the Jews. On the other hand there are other passages in the New Testament where 'God' is used of Jesus, notably John 1: 1–18, and probably Acts 20: 28, where we should read, 'the church of God, which he won for himself by his own blood'. Not many years later than the time the Pastorals were probably written, Ignatius writes quite confidently 'our God Jesus Christ' (in his letter to the Church in Rome III, 3). Again, if we follow here the translation in the N.E.B. footnote, we must suppose that the author was expecting the appearance of God the Father, which is quite contrary to all New Testament usage. We may add that, according to several New Testament writers, Jesus *is* the *splendour* of the Father; see 2 Cor. 4: 6, and especially James 2: 1, where the literal translation is 'believing as you do in our Lord Jesus Christ, the splendour'. It is quite possible that the author uses this particular formula here in conscious opposition to the emperor cult. The emperor was addressed as both God and Saviour, and he had his 'appearance' also. When we consider this tendency in the New Testament to describe Jesus as God, we can understand why the Church later on had to work out the doctrine of the Trinity.

14. The first half of this verse seems to be based on the LXX translation of Ps. 130: 7–9, which we may render as follows:

> For with the Lord is mercy
> and a great *ransoming* with him,
> and he will *ransom* Israel
> from all her *wickedness*.

The words printed in italics are connected with words in
Titus 2: 14. Compare also 1 John 1: 9, where the language
seems to be derived from the same Psalm, 'he is just, and may
be trusted to forgive our sins and cleanse us from every kind
of wrong'. The phrase *a . . . people marked out for his own*
comes from Deut. 14: 2 and Exod. 19: 5 'a peculiar treasure
unto me from among all peoples'.

eager to do good. Compare 1 Pet. 3: 13, 'devoted to what is
good', where 'devoted to' translates the same word in Greek
as *eager to* here. In his other letters the author does not show a
very keen interest in the Old Testament, so it seems very
likely that this passage was not composed by him but is
quoted from current liturgical material. ✶

THE CONSEQUENCES OF THE INCARNATION

These, then, are your themes; urge them and argue them. 15
And speak with authority: let no one slight you.

Remind them to be submissive to the government and **3**
the authorities, to obey them, and to be ready for any
honourable form of work; to slander no one, not to 2
pick quarrels, to show forbearance and a consistently
gentle disposition towards all men.

For at one time we ourselves in our folly and obstinacy 3
were all astray. We were slaves to passions and pleasures
of every kind. Our days were passed in malice and envy;
we were odious ourselves and we hated one another. But 4
when the kindness and generosity of God our Saviour
dawned upon the world, then, not for any good deeds of 5
our own, but because he was merciful,he saved us through

the water of rebirth and the renewing power of the Holy
6 Spirit. For he sent down the Spirit upon us plentifully
7 through Jesus Christ our Saviour, so that, justified by his
grace, we might in hope become heirs to eternal life.
8 These are words you may trust.

Such are the points I should wish you to insist on. Those
who have come to believe in God should see that they
engage in honourable occupations, which are not only
honourable in themselves, but also useful to their fellow-
9 men. But steer clear of foolish speculations, genealogies,
quarrels, and controversies over the Law; they are un-
profitable and pointless.

10 A heretic should be warned once, and once again; after
11 that, have done with him, recognizing that a man of that
sort has a distorted mind and stands self-condemned in his
sin.

* We have headed this passage 'The Consequences of the
Incarnation' because, on the whole, Christian conduct is
shown as being a consequence of *the kindness and generosity
of God our Saviour* (verse 4), whereas on the whole in the
previous section, the action of God in Christ is presented in
the light of its purpose.

2: 15. *let no one slight you*. There seems to be no particular
reason why anyone should, as Titus, unlike Timothy, could
not be represented as young and nervous. See 1 Cor. 16: 10,
'If Timothy comes, see that you put him at his ease'. Did the
author perhaps forget for a moment that Paul is supposed to
be addressing Titus and not Timothy? See 1 Tim. 4: 12,
'Let no one slight you because you are young'.

3: 1. *Remind them to be submissive to the government and to the
authorities*. There are three passages in the New Testament
where obedience to the authorities is encouraged. The other
two are Rom. 13: 1–10 and 1 Pet. 2: 13–17. The latter is worth

quoting, as it gives the fullest picture: 'Submit yourselves to every human institution for the sake of the Lord, whether to the sovereign as supreme, or to the governor as his deputy for the punishment of criminals and the commendation of those who do right. For it is the will of God that by your good conduct you should put ignorance and stupidity to silence. Live as free men; not however as though your freedom were there to provide a screen for wrongdoing, but as slaves in God's service. Give due honour to everyone: love to the brotherhood, reverence to God, honour to the sovereign.' Obviously the early Christians needed clear guidance on this urgent question; when Paul wrote, there was as yet little threat of official opposition to Christianity on the part of the rulers. When the author of 1 Peter wrote, persecution was already beginning. At the time of writing of the Pastorals, there seems to be no hint of persecution, but we may conjecture that relations with the government were beginning to be difficult.

3. This list of vices indulged in before the time of conversion is reminiscent of 2 Tim. 3: 2–4 (see the notes on that passage). Here too we have a list probably based on Rom. 1: 21–31, but it does not follow it as closely as does the list in 2 Timothy.

4. *the kindness and generosity of God our Saviour*. The two words *kindness* and *generosity* are so frequently used in Emperor worship that they may be borrowed from an inscription in honour of one of the emperors. At least it is very likely that the author uses them in deliberate challenge to the cult of the emperors.

5. *not for any good deeds of our own*, literally 'not because of any deeds in righteousness which we have done' (not a phrase of Paul's). We gain the impression of a writer who is anxious to preserve Paul's rejection of salvation by works, while not exactly understanding what Paul meant by righteousness.

he saved us through the water of rebirth and the renewing power of the Holy Spirit. The reference is of course to baptism, but the language is peculiar. The nearest parallel in the New Testament is Eph. 5: 25–6, 'Christ also loved the church and gave himself up for it, to consecrate it, cleansing it by water and word'. The same word *loutron* (literally 'washing') occurs in both passages; the N.E.B. translates it in both passages simply as 'water'. The word translated *rebirth* occurs elsewhere in the New Testament only in Matt. 19: 28, where it is translated 'the world that is to be'. It is a word that has wide non-Christian associations: Philo uses it of the renewal of the world after the flood, and the Stoics used it of the renewal of the world after the destruction by fire which they believed would strike the world periodically. Some scholars think the word was borrowed from the mystery religions, but others maintain that it was used in Judaism, and therefore can be applied to baptism in an eschatological sense; that is, baptism is the means of entry into the new age which came with the coming of Christ. The meaning of the Greek is not clear: the translation in the text suggests that baptism and the giving of the Spirit are distinct. The rendering in the N.E.B. footnote is 'the water of rebirth and of renewal by the Holy Spirit', which would identify baptism with the giving of the Holy Spirit. This on the whole seems the more likely meaning. This entire passage is closely paralleled by 1 Pet. 1: 3, 'Praise be to the God and Father of our Lord Jesus Christ, who in his mercy gave us new birth into a living hope by the resurrection of Jesus Christ from the dead'. This resemblance makes it all the more likely that we are here dealing with an extract from a baptismal liturgy.

6. *For he sent down the Spirit upon us plentifully.* Does this refer to the baptism of each individual Christian, or does it refer to Christ's baptism of the whole Church through his death and resurrection, which is apparently the meaning of Eph. 5: 25–6? Probably to both. The author is using a quotation which he applies to the Christian's baptism, but it may originally have referred to the baptism of the Church by Christ.

8. *These are words you may trust.* We encounter the last of the 'faithful words'. They must surely refer to what has gone before, especially as we suspect a liturgical formula here.

engage in honourable occupations. This was a genuine problem in the early Church. Could Christians serve in the army? What about Christian female slaves who were concubines?

Those who have come to believe in God means Christians, though the phrase would also cover Jews. The translation in the N.E.B. footnote is possible: 'should make it their business to practise virtue. These precepts are good in themselves and useful to society.' But it gives so trite and obvious a sense that one would prefer to credit the author with the sentiments conveyed in the N.E.B. text.

9. Almost identical with 1 Tim. 1: 4; 4: 7. The only new feature is *controversies over the Law*, which certainly implies the presence of a Jewish element in the false teaching.

10. *A heretic should be warned. . . .* It is not quite certain whether the word carries all the later implications of 'heretic', i.e. one who has formally been adjudged as holding a doctrine incompatible with traditional Christianity and who is therefore excommunicated. The custom of warning a trouble-maker twice before taking disciplinary action is a Jewish one, and is witnessed to in the early Church in Matt. 18: 15–17, where three warnings are to be given; but the first is perhaps purely informal.

11. *a distorted mind and stands self-condemned.* This is wholly in line with the rest of the Pastorals, where false teachers are abused and denounced rather than argued with. Paul, on the other hand, argues with opponents and refutes them. ✻

AN EXTRACT FROM A GENUINE LETTER OF PAUL

When I send Artemas to you, or Tychicus, make haste to 12 join me at Nicopolis, for that is where I have determined to spend the winter. Do your utmost to help Zenas the 13 lawyer and Apollos on their travels, and see that they are

14 not short of anything. And our own people must be taught to engage in honest employment to produce the necessities of life; they must not be unproductive.

15   All who are with me send you greetings. My greetings to those who are our friends in truth. Grace be with you all!

✲ We adopt the view that verses 12–13 are a fragment of a genuine letter of Paul's chiefly because of the unlikelihood that anyone should invent these particular details.

12. *Artemas.* Only mentioned here. One scholar makes the intriguing suggestion that his full name was Artemidorus, 'gift of Artemis', and that this connects him with Ephesus, the centre of the cult of Artemis (see Acts 19: 23–41).

Tychicus. See note on 2 Tim. 4: 12. He is connected with Colossae.

Nicopolis. One can identify no fewer than seven towns called Nicopolis in the ancient world; but it is very likely that Nicopolis in Epirus, north-western Greece, is intended here. In Rom. 15: 19, as we have seen, Paul tells us that the gospel had already reached Illyricum, which was actually further from Paul's starting-point than was Nicopolis. At any time, therefore, in his missionary service, Paul might have decided to winter in Nicopolis. We do not even know how he reached Illyricum. It is thus possible to regard this tiny fragment of a letter as belonging to any period in Paul's life between his first meeting with Apollos (Acts 18: 24) and his first imprisonment.

13. *Zenas the lawyer.* The word for *lawyer* is that used for the experts in Jewish law in the Gospels. But it is unlikely that this sort of description would be used for anyone outside Palestine, so it is better to take it in its ordinary secular sense of legal expert.

Apollos: the learned Jew of Alexandria, who was instructed in Christianity by Prisca and Aquila in Ephesus, who subsequently paid a visit to Corinth, and who was in Ephesus when Paul wrote his First Letter to the Corinthians. Many people think he is the author of the Letter to Hebrews. It seems unlikely that any Christian in Ephesus would need to be urged to help Apollos; when we put this fact together with the mention of Tychicus, we have a slight indication that this fragment of Paul's letter may have been preserved not in Ephesus but Colossae. In discussing the evidence for 2 Tim. 4 we came to a similar conclusion.

14. Here, we suggest, the fragment ends. In this verse we seem to meet again the style of the author of the Pastorals. See 3: 8, *engage in honourable occupations*; precisely the same phrase in Greek has been given two different translations by the N.E.B. in the course of seven verses.

15. If the ending had been genuinely Paul's one would have expected more personal greetings. ✳

✳   ✳   ✳   ✳   ✳   ✳   ✳   ✳   ✳   ✳   ✳   ✳   ✳

THE PASTORAL LETTERS TODAY

If we want at the end to sum up the value of the Pastoral letters, we may say that it is mainly to be found today in two features. First, they give us very useful evidence about the working of the Christian Church, probably in Asia Minor, probably at the very beginning of the second century. They show us the Church at worship, which we do not find in many other writings of the New Testament; and they show us a church leader grappling with the problems that beset the Church of his day—not by any means the same problems as Paul faced. Secondly, they encourage us by showing us an example of Christian faithfulness: the author was trying to maintain the original Christian witness; he was trying to be faithful to Christ and to Christ's Church. The fact that the Church still exists today shows that his efforts were not in vain.

A NOTE ON COMMENTARIES

We are fortunate in that three excellent commentaries have recently been published in English, all intended for students of undergraduate level. They are as follows:

C. K. Barrett. *The Pastoral Epistles* (Oxford, 1963)
> He refers to the Greek quite often, but his work can be used by those who do not know Greek.

J. N. D. Kelly. *A Commentary on the Pastoral Epistles* (in Black's New Testament Commentaries, London, 1963)
> Most informative, particularly on the background of the early Church. He takes the view that Paul wrote all three letters, an argument that did not carry conviction to the present writer at least.

A. R. C. Leaney. *The Epistles to Timothy, Titus, and Philemon* (in the Torch Commentary Series, London, 1960)
> Its usefulness is only limited by the shortness which space imposed on the author.

An older commentary of outstanding value is

B. S. Easton. *The Pastoral Epistles* (London, 1948)
> Full of valuable information, marred only by a determination to put the letters as late as the time of Marcion, and a refusal to admit any genuine information about Paul at all.

Other commentaries which might be mentioned are:

D. Guthrie. *The Pastoral Epistles* (London, 1957)
> A scholarly attempt to maintain the traditional authorship.

E. F. Scott. *The Pastoral Epistles* (Moffatt New Testament Commentaries, London, 1936)
> Sound common sense and good scholarship.

E. F. Brown. *The Pastoral Epistles* (Westminster Commentaries London, 1917)
> Written by a missionary in India, and therefore containing some valuable insights. But his outlook is very much that of the nineteenth-century paternalistic missionary. Paul and Timothy are portrayed as if they were a senior missionary of a British missionary society and his newly arrived colleague.

INDEX

INDEX